THE MEANING AND MESSAGE

OF

THE FOURTH GOSPEL

THE MEANING AND MESSAGE

OF

THE FOURTH GOSPEL

A STUDY IN THE APPLICATION OF
JOHANNINE CHRISTIANITY TO THE
PRESENT THEOLOGICAL SITUATION

BY

C. J. WRIGHT, B.D., Ph.D.

AUTHOR OF "MIRACLE IN HISTORY AND IN MODERN THOUGHT";
TUTOR IN SYSTEMATIC THEOLOGY AND THE PHILOSOPHY OF
RELIGION IN DIDSBURY COLLEGE, MANCHESTER

LONDON
HODDER & STOUGHTON LIMITED
1933

56600

Made and Printed in Great Britain for HODDER AND STOUGHTON LTD.
by THE ABERDEEN UNIVERSITY PRESS LTD., Aberdeen

TO

MY FATHER AND MOTHER

PREFACE

THIS book has been written almost un-
awares. A few weeks ago I had no
intention to write anything for publication
on the Fourth Gospel. Like every other
student of the Christian religion, I had
pondered on this "divine" Gospel, and in
my lectures have sought to guide others
to a right interpretation. Difficulties raised
by students for the Christian ministry have
recalled to me what I myself felt when I sat
as a learner in the theological and New Testament lecture-rooms some twenty years ago.
But it had not come within any conscious
purpose of mine to publish anything on the
subject.

Recently it was suggested to me by a
friend that I had something to say upon
the meaning and message of this Gospel.
I thought I might do this in a brief Quarterly
article. But, somewhat to my own surprise,
in the course of a few weeks the following
pages had appeared, in substantially their
present form. After many critical self-com-

munings I have felt it well not to alter the direct and spontaneous—though not, I trust, unconsidered—mode of expression and of presentation which are manifest in what follows.

I have not sought either to add another to the many able discussions on the linguistic and critical issues involved, or to write a Commentary. My intention has been two-fold: to maintain firstly that the Johannine author's penetrating insight into the religious consciousness of the Historic Jesus is a clue to the author's *meaning*, and, secondly, that this insight is of abiding value in any adequate apologetic for Christianity. Underlying this twofold aim is the conviction that the Fourth Gospel focusses at a vivid and burning point many of the contentious issues of modern religious thought, and, therefore, that it is strikingly relevant to our own day.

To my friend, Dr. W. L. Wardle, who has very kindly read through the proofs, I wish to express my warm thanks.

C. J. WRIGHT.

DIDSBURY COLLEGE,
MANCHESTER.

CONTENTS

9

M Y title indicates the two issues with which I wish here to deal. I say " two issues," for while the " meaning " and the " message " are interpenetrative, it is well nevertheless to distinguish them. By the " meaning " of the Gospel I wish to deal with the *author's* meaning : here obviously the inquiry is a historical one, involving interpretative or exegetical issues. By the " message " of the Gospel I wish to deal with its *abiding* message : here obviously the inquiry leads away beyond a mere discussion of what the author meant, involving the whole question of its truth and of its significance and place in a Christian statement. In order to perceive the distinctness, yet interpenetrativeness, of the two issues, it will suffice to say, on the one hand, that, conceivably, when we discovered an author's meaning we should find in it no truth or value for ourselves ; and, on the other hand, that it would be

impossible to maintain that we could be justified in holding that the abiding message of
a book could be something far removed from
the author's own thought. My own thesis
here is that when we have discovered the
author's own meaning we shall find therein
a message of eternal value.

For the last generation and more, many
of the Church's theological teachers have
manifested a considerable *malaise* when they
had to confront the central issues for thought
raised by this Gospel. In their theological
constructions they could neither use this
Gospel nor ignore it. Such use as was made
of it was frequently lame, hesitating, apologetic. Yet the Gospel was such as could
not be ignored : greatness was written on
the very face of it. To read it was to breathe
the air of the eternities ; to meditate upon it
was to find satisfaction for the deepest and
highest within. Many of the Church's most
honest-minded preachers have been in similar
case. With what they regarded as the pro-
foundest of the Gospels before them, they were
often debarred from expounding it by lurk-
ing uncertainties and hesitations as to its

historical truth. The Fourth Gospel has been both a puzzle and a glory; but we could not unfeignedly rejoice in its glory until we had, to some degree at least, seen our way through its puzzle. Thus, theologians have often used it with "gêne," and preachers have used it less than they intuitively felt they ought and they might.

CHAPTER I

THE MEANING

FIRST, let us consider the *meaning* of the Gospel, and some of the difficulties in arriving thereat.

The main difficulty, let it be said at once, has been in respect of its precise historical character. Both in regard to incident and in regard to the portraiture of the mind of Jesus there is much here that is not in the Synoptic Gospels. And if, as the result of our study of the Synoptic problem, we are led to conclude that, in the main, a soundly historical outline of the life of Jesus can be deduced from these three Gospels, are we not necessarily compelled to relinquish as unhistorical much of the incident and much of the self-revelation of the Central Figure which this Gospel contains ? And having reached this rejective conclusion, does not the rejection of the traditional authorship immediately follow ? For how is it possible to conceive that Gospels written by those who were not apostles are more to be relied upon historically than the Gospel which purports to be written by one who was of that inner and privileged company ?

Nor do we escape this difficulty by suggesting, as was at one time so frequently done, that the differences relate only to matters which may be amplificatory of the Synoptic outline. It is true that there is much in the Fourth Gospel which is a valuable supplement to the narrative of the Synoptists—for example, in the record of the ministry in Judæa. Nevertheless, there are differences in the two accounts which are not susceptible of a merely " supplementary " explanation. For such a narrated incident as the raising of Lazarus cannot with complete candour be regarded as merely amplificatory. On it, according to the Fourth Gospel, hangs much of the psychological motivations which lead to the tragedy, or glory, of the Crucifixion. Or, to give another and, from some points of view, an even more important illustration, the static, unchanging, developed inner consciousness of Jesus as portrayed by the fourth evangelist does not cohere with the genetic or developing inner consciousness as deduced by nearly all modern students from the Synoptic narratives. Cæsarea Philippi is probably more than just an open avowal before the disciples of what had been his own " Messianic secret " ; it, we are constrained to feel, represents a culminating and determining stage in the fruition of his self-consciousness and of his conception of mission. There is, however, little or nothing of this in the Fourth Gospel. Not only is it that there Jesus guards no " Messianic secret "— he, indeed, proclaims from the first his Messianic vocation—but also, the whole inner consciousness of Jesus seems to be at its apex from the beginning.

THE AUTHOR.

I have instanced these two differences— and they are without doubt the crucial ones— in order to confront at once what has been generally felt to be the main difficulty in ascertaining the meaning of the Gospel. And obviously—though this is not my real concern here—the question of authorship is involved. It is perhaps sufficient to say that the question of historicity and the question of authorship are interpenetrative issues ; and it is not altogether easy to determine whether the problem of authorship should be approached through the problem of historicity, or *vice versa*. Suffice it to say that, when we ponder all the factors involved, the former seems the only really satisfactory method of approach. In other words, the question of authorship can be best approached through the question of the interpretation of the Gospel itself. The authorship of the Gospel is subsidiary to the interpretation of its essential character. I do not think that in the light of the nature of the Gospel itself the external evidence for the Apostolic authorship is decisive. And it is in large measure this method of approach that has led nearly all modern students of the Gospel to renounce the apostolic authorship. Added to these differences is the fact of the author's dependence on the Synoptists : and this dependence seems to many a crucial argument against the Johannine authorship. Who the author of this Gospel, as we now have it, was we shall probably never know : as we shall probably never know who was the author of the Epistle to the Hebrews. All we can say is, with Professor Maurice Goguel, that he is " le grand anonyme dont la personalité transparaît dans les écrits johanniques."[1]   The most likely conjecture is that he was the Elder John of Ephesus, to whom Papias refers in the familiar passage cited by Eusebius.[2]

---

[1] *Revue d'histoire et de philosophie religieuses*, Mai-Juin, 1931, p. 189.

[2] Eusebius, *H.E.*, iii, 39.   The passage is as follows : " ' But if I met with anyone who had been a follower of the elders anywhere, I made it a point to inquire what were the declarations of the elders : what was said by Andrew, Peter, or Philip : what by Thomas, James, John, Matthew, or any other of the disciples of our Lord : what is said by Aristion, and the Elder John, disciples of the Lord ; for I do not think that I derived so much benefit from books as from the living voice of those that are still surviving.' Where it is also proper to observe that the name of John is twice mentioned (as Eusebius himself continues) : the former of which he mentions with Peter and James and Matthew, and the other apostles ; evidently meaning the evangelist. But in a separate point of his discourse, he ranks the other John with the rest not included in the number of apostles, placing Aristion before him. He distinguishes him

To acquiesce, however, in the judgement
that the author is anonymous does not mean
that we acquiesce in a complete agnosticism
as to his characteristics, or even as to his
relation to some historical source for his
portraiture of Jesus. Obviously, such an
agnosticism is incompatible with any endeavour to understand the Gospel. Every
interpretation of the Gospel involves some
judgement as to the nature of the author's
mind, as to what he was seeking to do, and
as to the materials with which he had to work.
If, for example, no historical reliance be placed
upon the Gospel—both as to its incident and
as to the portraiture of the mind of the historic Jesus—it is clear that involved in this
interpretation there is the theory that the

plainly by the name of Elder. So that it is here proved
that the statement of those is true who assert that there
were two of the same name in Asia, that there were also
two tombs in Ephesus, and that both are called John
even to this day ; which it is particularly necessary to
observe."

The fact that there were two Johns in Ephesus is
evidenced also in the *Apostolic Constitutions*, vii, 4,
where we are told that as bishops of Ephesus, there
were " Timotheus ordained by Paul, and John by John."

author had neither personal historical re-
miniscences to expound, nor data derived at
first hand from an apostolic source. And
if, for example, as we shall seek to maintain,
there is sound basis in history for the unveiling
of the inner consciousness of Jesus given to
us in this Gospel, obviously there is involved
in such a judgement the theory that the
author had either had personal association
with Jesus or was very dependent on one
who was of the inner band.

We do not, therefore, settle the issues by
declaring that the internal character of the
Gospel decides the question of authorship.
For the real question is : What *is* its internal
character ? Is it, for example, primarily a
theological or metaphysical interpretation of
a Jesus who died nearly a hundred years
before the author wrote ? Is it, to use the
words of a distinguished British interpreter
of the Gospel, that " metaphysical categories
have assumed the place of the moral and religious categories of primitive Christianity " ?
Is it that " the purely religious view (of the
Gospel) is overlaid and obscured by the conception of Christianity as a speculative system,

which makes its primary appeal to the logical intelligence " ? [1] In my own view this is a mis-reading of the essential nature and purpose of the Gospel. Yet it is obvious that such an interpretation as that to which I have referred will itself decide the question of authorship, and, so, of date. Granted, there-fore, the indecisive nature of the external evidence, we have yet to recognise that the " decisive " nature of the internal character-istics depends upon their interpretation. These characteristics are decisive ; but the real question is : What *are* they ?

It is well that I should here frankly say that my own interpretation of the essential nature of the Gospel involves the following kind of author. First, he was a Jew : I take this as indisputable, whatever view of the nature of the Gospel we accept. Secondly, in his earlier life he had lived in Palestine, and had there, probably in Jerusalem, in the closing days of the Master's life been brought into intimate personal contact with Jesus. Thirdly, he had, later in his life in Ephesus, been a close friend or disciple of John the Apostle—the

[1] E. F. Scott, *The Fourth Gospel*, p. 256 and p. 98.

" beloved disciple," as I believe, of the Gospel
—with whose mind he had singular congenital
affinity. It was after the Apostle had de-
parted this life that our author sat down to
convey in dramatic narrative form the secret
of that unique Life on which he had meditated
so long. To this meditation he brought a
mind of a singularly penetrating character.
It was not so much systematic as unitive.
Unlike Paul, this writer had not to write in the
stress of difficult practical situations. His
thinking was not done to the order of the perplexing intellectual and administrative issues
confronting the Church. One such doctrinal
issue had appeared on the horizon—I refer
to the Docetic peril. But it is, on the whole,
true to say that this Gospel is the ripe product
of a mind whose interior unity has come,
not by striving without and crying within,
but under the inspiration of a penetrating
spiritual insight.

It is not with any intention of disparaging
the great mind of Paul that I contrast our
author with him. In Paul we see a man
thinking ; in the Fourth Gospel we see the
unified and completed *thought*. In the one

we see insight in process of being fused by
thought ; in the other we see thought already
fused by insight. Each was in the right
and best sense " apologetic "—" These things,"
says our author, in what are probably the
last words of the original Gospel, " are written
that ye may believe—πιστεύητε, may continue in believing—that Jesus is the Christ,
the Son of God, and that believing ye may
have life in his name " (xx. 31). This
apologetic, however, in the case of the
Johannine author, is not so much argumenta-
tive or reasoned as declaratory. The writer
believes that the best apologetic for Christianity is just to state the truth as he himself
sees it.

The Gospel is written more to express insight than to set forth arguments. The author
is content to believe that those who have
eyes to see will see, and ears to hear will hear.
His is not the desperate endeavour to answer
every question in heaven and on earth, nor
does he hope to enforce belief by the compre-
hensiveness and cogency of his presentation.
He will leave, therefore, many questions to
be asked, and many issues to be raised. If,

then, we venture to call his purpose an *apologetic* one, it has to be clearly noted that it has little in common with the endeavours that inspired much of the literature which has gone by that name. When he writes he is not haunted by the thought of the possible sceptical answers to what he says. He does not, therefore, trim his sails to the point of complete safety. He does not say, and then half-unsay.

I have frequently thought that some of the opening words of the famous discourse of the Savoyard Vicar in Rousseau's *Émile* are deeply expressive of the type of apologetic represented by the mind and spirit of the Johannine author. " Mon enfant, n'attendez de moi ni des discours savants ni de profonds raisonnements. Je ne suis pas un grand philosophe, et je me soucie peu de l'être. . . . Je ne veux pas argumenter avec vous, ni même tenter de vous convaincre ; il me suffit de vous exposer ce que je pense dans la sim-plicité de mon coeur. Consultez le vôtre durant mon discours ; c'est tout ce que je vous demande." Our author, however, was both more ardent and more luminous than the vicar of Savoie. It was what he *saw* and what he *felt,* as well as what he *thought,* in the depth of his mind that he sought to express. Tepid dispassionateness had no part or lot in him ; nor the nicely calculated more or less of correct rational discussion ; nor the exactitude and precision of scientific history.

Probably, further, when he wrote he was thinking almost solely of the children of the Church. It was in order that they might *continue in believing* that he wrote. He pre-supposes some belief in his readers.

THE CLUE TO THE GOSPEL.

What, then, is the truth as he sees it ? It is, as I have suggested already, the truth about the inner mind and consciousness of Jesus.

This, he sees with intuitive penetration, is the really important thing about Jesus. Our Lord's conscious relation to God, from which sprang his knowledge of the Divine Will and of his own mission, is the real kernel of the truth about him, and, therefore, the real basis for every adequate Christian apolo-getic, and, certainly, for any defensible Chris-tology. I would venture to call the Johannine author *the historian of the consciousness of Jesus.*

Now, if this method of interpretation of the Gospel is sound, it must have an answer to two main questions. First, is there historical substantiation in the dependable Synoptic narrative for the unique conscious relation which this writer portrays Jesus as having with God ? And, second, what are we to make of the indisputable historical incompatibilities, in regard to this very issue, between this Gospel and the generally accepted Synoptic outline ?

1. *The Fourth Gospel in essential agreement with the Synoptic Gospels on this issue.*—In considering the first of these issues, it is obviously necessary to set forth what precisely is his teaching about the mind and, especially, the inner consciousness of Jesus, and to place this alongside the authentic teaching of the Synoptic Gospels.

At the outset it should be clearly noted— and the point is often overlooked, to the misinterpretation of the author's meaning—that in the Fourth Gospel the Central Figure is subject to characteristic human experiences.

The thesis that the Gospel is allegory and nothing but allegory, or that the Figure portrayed is a dogmatic abstraction, is a too facile theory which fails to confront the whole intricate and many-sided problem which the work presents. The writer has before his mind from the beginning a real historical Jesus, who was flesh of our flesh and had human susceptibilities and limitations such as we ourselves know. Whatever connotation was given in his thought to the "Word"— λόγος—at any rate "the Word became flesh and dwelt among us." He knew what weariness of body was (iv. 6), the grief which has its outlet in tears (xi. 35), the distress of mind when an intimate associate is seen to be a traitor (xiii. 21), the physical thirst which accompanies acute bodily anguish and nervous tension (xix. 28). At least, there is no room in this Gospel for Docetism. Further, the Jesus of this Gospel is in all things dependent upon the Father. His "authority to execute judgment" is from the Father; he can do nothing of himself (v. 27, 30). He prays to the Father (xiv. 16; xvi. 26; xvii. 9, 15, 20). His sustenance is in doing

the will of Him that sent him (iv. 34). He
is in the world not to do his own will but the
will of Him that sent him (vi. 38). It is the
Father indwelling in him who does his works
(xiv. 10). His knowledge has come to him
as taught by the Father (viii. 28) ; nor is
there anything in the Gospel to suggest that
to the writer this " knowledge " is what is
usually called " omniscience."

It is perhaps hardly necessary to say that
all this is coherent with the Synoptic portraiture. It is going too far, I think, to suggest,
as has sometimes been done, that the human
characteristics of Jesus are more emphasised
in this Gospel than in the others [1]—the substratum of truth in such a suggestion is that
by contrast with the central emphasis of the
Gospel these very human experiences stand
out with unique vividness. Nevertheless, the

[1] See, e.g. F. C. Burkitt's *Gospel History and its
Transmission*, p. 233, where he says that " in no early
Christian document is the real humanity of Jesus so
emphasised as in the Fourth Gospel " ; also, Streeter
in *The Four Gospels* who says that the Johannine author
" to an extent unparalleled in the Synoptics, emphasises
the susceptibility of Christ to purely physical and simple
human experience " (p. 387).

fourth Gospel author did find it necessary
to his purpose to give these details ; and from
this I can only conclude that before his mind
as he wrote is the truly human historical
Jesus of the Synoptic Gospels. He gave
these details in fidelity to the Human Figure
he remembered and had so long meditated
upon. The Jesus he portrays and whose
secret he seeks to unfold is no theological
abstraction. Doubtless, also, a growing
Gnostic and Docetic tendency of thought
in the Church accentuated his concern for
this *human* emphasis. If I may dare to put
it so, he was anchored to the historical.
The historical Jesus was as much his concern
as he was the concern of the Synoptists.
Indeed, from one point of view, this was an
even more necessary concern to him, for the
simple reason that without the real historical
Human Figure his central thesis falls to the
ground. That thesis was no other than that
the Divine *Logos* had been incarnate in time
and place. I leave till later the question as
to what precisely he meant when he said
that "*the word* became flesh and dwelt
among us," in the meantime merely stressing

the fact that at least he meant that there had been a definite historical figure to whom these words referred. On the hypothesis that the author has not before his mind a specific person, one who in the flesh dwelt among men, there is what I can only regard as the preposterous theory that this author enunciates a thesis which he himself holds cannot be substantiated. There are various interpretations of the Gospel which make the author an inner or psychological contradiction ; but no theory which makes him so fantastic a self-contradiction as this one.

But now—and this is the main issue—what has he to say about Jesus's conscious relation to God ?

The overmastering conception of the Gospel is that Jesus has a unique conscious filial relation to God. Through the whole terrain of the Gospel shines this central illuminating beam. It is like the shaft of light which pierces the clouds, descending to this very earth in which, bounded by time and space, we dwell. It flows from eternity into time, from the infinite to the finite, breaking through the encompassing barriers of our mortality. I am myself fully convinced from long meditation upon this Gospel that it is *the main thing* our author wanted to say. And I am further convinced that it was not any *new* thing he was saying : but only that by his own penetrating, intuitive insight he saw, with an intoxicating clarity which almost blinded him to the significance of historical exactitude in incident and word of the Master, what the others had seen only fitfully and sporadically. In other words, I am convinced that what he saw was fundamentally historically true. This complete certitude of God, expressed under the figure of unique filial relationship to God, was the real secret of the whole life of Jesus, the one key which opens to us the record of his words and his deeds.

The exigencies of space and of my own purpose forbid my elucidation of this issue with the minute and detailed examination of the Gospel which it would require in a critical treatise. But consider such passages as the following : " My Father worketh hitherto and I work," " The Son can do nothing of himself, but what he seeth the Father doing," " I am come in my Father's name " (v.

3

17, 19, 43) ; " For this is the will of my Father, that every one that beholdeth the Son, and believeth on him, should have eternal life " (vi. 40) ; " Ye are from beneath ; I am from above : ye are of this world ; I am not of this world," " Verily, verily, I say unto you, Before Abraham was, I am " (viii. 23, 58) ; " I and the Father are one " (x. 30) ; " If he called them gods, unto whom the word of God came (and the word of God cannot be broken), say ye of him whom the Father sanctified and sent into the world, Thou blasphemest ; because I said, I am the Son of God ? " (x. 35-6) ; " Believe me that I am in the Father and the Father in me " (xiv. 11) ; " Father, the hour is come ; glorify thy Son, that the Son may glorify thee " (xvii. 1).

These passages, to which many others might be added, reveal that to the author of the Fourth Gospel Jesus had a unique and perfect conscious filial relation to God. I leave for the moment the very important question for theology as to precisely *how* this filial relation is to be interpreted, and go on to show that this is true to the Synoptic portraiture of Jesus.

not a public proclamation to which they were
called to yield an unenlightened assent.
" Thou " said to him the inward voice, which
yet he knew to be from above, " art my
beloved Son, in thee I am well pleased." The
very fact, surely, that here at the beginning
of his ministry the three Synoptic writers
place a record which tells of an experience
within his consciousness whereby he becomes
convinced of a unique filial relation to God
indicates some insight on their part that this
consciousness was the key to the whole
ministry of Jesus. That which dominates
everything in the Fourth Gospel is here set
forth as the inspiring, directing and controlling
beginning. Further, in these Gospels it is
the foundation on which rests the whole of
the after-teaching and task of Jesus. The
fact that he came to accept with assured
conviction an ideal Messianic vocation presupposes a signal certitude of God. It is not
the former which explains the latter, it is
the latter which alone gives adequate psychological explanation of the former. In
other words, his knowledge of God is not an
inference from his sense of vocation ; it is

the *fount* of that sense of vocation. Further, it was only because he himself knew God as Father that he came to teach his disciples to call him Father. The figure, which by a natural inevitability expressed his unique and direct consciousness of God, was used to convey to them the truth which ought to be theirs as well. Here may I suggest that the difference between the " *my* Father " with which he himself addresses God, and the " *our* Father " with which he teaches his disciples to address God, has been the object of much singularly blind and uninspired argumentation. Into this difference by the dogmatists has been read a metaphysic of existence ; and, on the other hand, into it by the other type of rationalists—the rationalists in this case of the left—has been read the negation of any difference of experience between Jesus and ourselves. And so the shuttlecock has sped from right to left and left to right, as if the choice imposed was between a reading into the consciousness of Jesus the Christology of later dogmatics, *and* a denial of that unique consciousness itself. The plain fact, to those who have eyes to see, being that the figure

he used—the figure of Father—expressed *his own* knowledge of God, and not that of others ; and that he could only teach the disciples to call Him " Father " because he himself had seen and known Him as such. My point is that whatever metaphysic we reach must be reached on the basis of the facts—the chief fact here being Jesus's unique consciousness of God : such metaphysic must not be *read into* the basal fact of that consciousness. The differentiation of metaphysical status which, when it was reached by the Church, came to be determinative of Christological and Trinitarian formulations cannot, I am convinced, be attributed to the direct consciousness of Jesus. Rather, it must be regarded as a human, finite statement whose validity rests, not upon itself, but upon the validity of the experience to which it seeks to give formal and rational expression. This is not to deny the legitimacy and, from our human point of view, the necessity of some type of Christological and Trinitarian formulation. It is to maintain the basis in experience on which rests all such formulations, by which basis alone they have to be tested.

But to return to our historical issue. This unique consciousness of God possessed by Jesus is seen in such parables as that of the Husbandmen (Mk. xii. 1-11; Matt. xxi. 33-46; Lk. xx. 9-19), and of the Marriage Feast (Matt. xxii. 1-14; cp. Lk. xiv. 16-24) In the former the words, "He had yet one, a beloved son : he sent him last unto them saying, They will reverence my son," indicate so vivid and direct a sense of the presence of God that Jesus distinguished his own mission from that of the prophets who had preceded him—called in the parable "servants." Again, it is the *consciousness* which imposes the differentiation in figure ; it is not the differentiation in figure which imposes the consciousness. The road once more is from a unique certitude of God and of vocation to the use of metaphors which seek to express it ; the road is not from rigidly and dogmatically conceived metaphors to a consciousness which they are regarded as necessitating in an absolute manner.

This unique filial consciousness is perhaps most vividly and directly expressed in that famous, and sublime, Synoptic " Q " passage

which has occasioned so much, as I must feel, confused and confusing argumentation : " I thank Thee, O Father, Lord of heaven and earth, that Thou hast hidden these things from the wise and prudent, and hast revealed them to babes ; yea, Father, for so it was well-pleasing in Thy sight. All things are delivered to me of my Father, and no one knows the Son save the Father, or the Father save the Son, and he to whom the Son wills to reveal Him " (Matt. xi. 25-7 ; Lk. x. 21-2). The psychological reality throbbing behind these words is a unique certitude of God, and a unique certitude of vocation. That direct and immediate certitude expressed itself in language which can, on the one hand, be so facilely explained as arising from a metaphysical—or physical—inference which Jesus himself had drawn ; and which can, on the other hand, be so facilely explained away as " a bolt from the Johannine sky." I wish to say, to those who maintain the former view, that the metaphysical inference is ours, not that of Jesus—and this while believing that some type of metaphysical statement will always be necessary to our

minds as long as they dwell in the realm of
frail, finite mortality, encompassed as they
are by the " shades of the prison house " of
time and space. I wish to say to those
who maintain the latter view—my main contention in this part of my book—that the
utterance is neither of the nature of a " bolt,"
nor is " the Johannine sky " an unhistorical
dogma. There is the same over-arching sky
of ethical and spiritual sublimity in the Synoptists as in the Fourth Gospel ; and from that
sky descends, not an isolated " bolt," but
a steady stream of revealing light. Surely,
both clauses in this so striking utterance—
" striking," only because it is approached
with prepossessions, whether dogmatic or
negative prepossessions—flow naturally from
such an awareness of God as is manifest
throughout the whole evangelical narrative.
For myself, I can see no conclusive ground
for extirpating either one or the other of the
two clauses, which together form a naturally
harmonious unity. For, on the one hand,
such an intimate and direct consciousness
or knowledge of God gives Jesus the feeling
of certitude that he is known uniquely to

the Father ; and, on the other hand, such consciousness or knowledge carries with it a conviction that the Father is known uniquely to him, and that he, by this knowledge, is called to be a unique " revealer " of " all things " pertaining to the Kingdom. The mutual knowledge of friends should help to throw light on the mysterious depths of the consciousness behind these words. If I have a friend with whom I have perfect intimacy—and such an experience is rarer than could be wished—I have the conviction that my inmost mind is known to him as to no one else ; and I also have the conviction that his inmost mind is known to me as to no one else, and that I can thus interpret his thought and will—if necessary plead his cause—to those whose knowledge of him is superficial and blind. Such an illustration will be regarded as *essentially* invalid—all illustrations are *inadequate* to super-sensuous, spiritual consciousness—only to those who cannot believe that man can really *know* God. But to those who believe that a *knowledge* of God, and not just a *knowledge about* God, is possible the *knowledge* we have of our true friends, not just the physiological and psychological knowledge we have *about* them, will be seen to throw an illuminating beam upon this famous " Q " utterance of Jesus. If we do *not* believe that man can *know* God we shall *either* regard this saying as unhistorical, *or* we shall regard it as a " metaphysical " utterance of Jesus to which mere assent, and into which not personal insight, is demanded. In the first case, it will be regarded as a reading of later theological and speculative reflection into the Gospel narrative ; in the latter case this theological and speculative reflection will be attributed to the mind of Jesus himself. If we *do* believe that man can *know* God, we shall regard the saying as giving natural and fitting expression to the unique religious *knowledge* of God possessed by Jesus.

This unique consciousness of God possessed by Jesus is also clearly revealed in the prayer in the garden of Gethsemane (Mk. xiv. 36 ; Matt. xxvi. 39 ; Lk. xxii. 42) : " Abba, Father, all things are possible to Thee : remove this cup from me : howbeit not what I will, but what Thou wilt." There is here revealed such perfect trust and obedience as has no more

truly sublime expression in the Fourth Gospel—
a trust that triumphs over physical shrinking,
and, what is worse, the darkness of intellectual
perplexity. This trustful consciousness of
God penetrates through the blackness of the
Cross, where, according to Mark and Matthew,
he expresses himself in doubtlessly familiar
words from the twenty-second Psalm: " My
God, my God, why hast Thou forsaken me "
(Mk. xv. 34 ; Matt. xxvii. 46). Here again, as
I cannot but think, both the soteriological
dogmatists and the secularist dogmatists have
indulged in argumentation which has made
truth as but darkness. To the one, Jesus
drinks now the last drops of sin's penalty—
complete alienation, separation, from God ;
to the other, he now perceives that there is
no God at all. Surely, the meaning of the
words on the lips of Jesus is to be found in
the whole context of his mind and experience
at this time, and not either in the atonement
theory we want to have " proved," or in the
atheistic presupposition for which we want
to find a psychological buttress even in the
one who has taught the world to call God
" Father." And, in the light of that context,

we remember, first, the whole Psalm he quotes,
whose entirety of meaning was surely known
to himself : for the Psalmist still addresses
God as "*my*" even when he seems "forsaken" ; which shows to these who have
eyes to see that the "abandonment," "de-
sertion," "dereliction"—all these words have
been used in commentary and treatise—was
conceived as of no *absolute* character ; and,
further, the note of assurance and trust is
the undertone of the whole psalm and, at
the close, comes pealing through it. In the
light of that whole context of Jesus's experience at this time we remember, secondly,
the two utterances recorded only by Luke,
one as prior to the words being considered,
the other as later. In the first Jesus reveals
both perfect love for men and perfect faith in
God (Lk. xxiii. 34—omitted by several important MSS., among them B and D), "Father,
forgive them, for they know not what they
do" : in the second, Jesus breathes his last
physical breath with words of complete trustful certitude from another psalm (Ps. xxxi.
5) : "Father, into Thy hands I commend
my spirit" (Lk. xxiii. 46).

Further, there is very much in the Synoptic narratives which, while it does not make explicit avowal of unique spiritual knowledge of the Father nevertheless involves it, or springs naturally from it. Mark tells us at the beginning of his Gospel that the hearers of Jesus were astonished at his teaching ; " for he taught them as one who has authority, and not as the scribes " (i. 22). Whence flowed this self-evidencing authority of his speech ? Whence, but from the whole depth of a personality which was grounded in a unique spiritual knowledge of God ? He did not quote even such " authoritative " words as those of the Old Testament to " prove " what he had to say. He, instead, referred to the truth that was in them, in order to lead the thought of his hearers back to the one source of truth which welled up in himself. " Ye have heard that it was said to them of old time . . . but I say unto you. . . ." Behind all the " authorities " he penetrated to the one Authority, speaking through those of old " in divers parts and by divers manners," but speaking in fullness and in directly-evidenced certitude within

the unplumbed depths of his own consciousness. And so his " I say unto you " was
not meant to direct a mere submissive, un-
inquiring and unillumined assent to what
he said, just because *he* said it. He sought
to elicit a personal insight, a personal trust,
a personal obedience. The only person who
at one and the same time speaks with absolute
conviction and yet does not seek to impose
his own convictions upon others is he who
himself rests upon the only Authority, namely,
reality evidencing itself within as truth.
The " dogmatist "—as he may be called,
in the technical sense of that term—rests
upon the *fact of having been told*, and upon the
way, or mode, by which he has been told. He
of whom the synoptists speak rested upon *the
fact of what was told*, and on *the way by which
what had been told evidenced itself within the
depths of his own consciousness and in the
whole outward terrain of his activities*. The
" miracle " of God's activity to him did not
rest on the *mode* or theory by which he conceived God ought to work, but on the fact
of that activity as it evidenced itself within
the whole depth and through the whole range

of his nature. The " miracle " of God's word
or speech to men did not depend to him upon
any mode or theory of " inspiration " such as
could be measured as satisfactory by a rigid,
traditionalist rationalism, but on the fact of
that word as the deep without calling unto
the deep within. And so he did not set up
another " standard " of Authority for his
brethren in addition to those they already
knew. The only real blasphemy in his eyes
was in refusing to follow the eternal values
when they were there. This is the " blasphemy against the Holy Spirit " which " hath
never forgiveness " (Mk. iii. 29 ; Lk. xii. 10 ;
Matt. xii. 32). All other denials are " for-
givable," for they may spring from sincere
and honest error : they may involve, for
instance, but the refusal to acquiesce before
the determined dogmatisms of men's " infallible authorities "—a refusal which has had
within it the seeds of humanity's truest and
deepest growth. Even, therefore, a " sin
against the Son of man " can be forgiven—
any and every denial except the denial that
love and truth and beauty are there to be
our guide and our stay, our light and our goal.

4

Coming from one who had pure and perfect fellowship with God, can such an attitude of freedom and absolute claim for the rights of personality be other than the supreme vindication that he was unique *son* of God ? It is the unique Son who can only be satisfied when others know and experience their own sonship. Those who masquerade as " sons " wish to perpetuate the delusion of spurious privilege by getting others to wear the formal badges of filial rank which have come down to themselves. Their appeal is not to Truth but to Pride—the frail human pride of which Shakespeare speaks :

> *proud man,*
> *Drest in a little brief authority,*
> *Most ignorant of what he's most assur'd.*

Be we not, indeed, children of Abraham ? or children of a privileged Sect ? Can we not trace our unbroken descents ? Can we not point to the certainty of our covenanted channels of grace, to our unmistakable apostolic successions, to our compact infallible dogmas ? Yes ! our title-deeds may be all in order. But the Unique Son is not satisfied with title-deeds. He calls for an inner life and an outer obedience which *themselves* claim the title. He calls for Reality; because he calls *from* Reality. He himself knew the perfect freedom of being God's Son. How then could he be satisfied with the spurious freedom of men's delusive pride? The Son wants men to be truly free—" if the Son shall make you free, ye shall be free indeed." The supreme vindication of the sonship of Jesus is in the fact that he could be content with nothing less in his fellows. This recognition of the *rights* of human personality, and, therefore, of the goal or *end* of personality on the part of Jesus, pervades the Synoptic record. It sprang from his own unclouded sonship.

It was this constant fellowship—this, if we may venture so to call it, ethical and spiritual solidarity—with the Father which compelled the Synoptists to portray one who was "more than a prophet." He whose perfection of realised sonship permitted him to say, not, "Thus saith the Lord," but " I say unto you," was indeed to them " a greater than Jonah " and " a greater than Solomon " (Matt. xii. 41-2 ; Lk. xi. 31-2).

From all this—and much might be added—
I conclude that when the author of the Fourth
Gospel ascribes to Jesus a unique, perfect
filial relation to God he is only saying what
the Synoptists had already said, even though
he says it with a dominating continuity of
emphasis and with features stamped by the
aptitudes and insights of his own mind.

2. *The "incompatibilities," on this very
issue, between the Fourth Gospel and the Synoptics, and how to be regarded.*—We now come
to consider the incompatibilities, and on this
very issue, between this Fourth Gospel and
the Synoptic statement. In discussing this,
it will be necessary to endeavour to interpret
in a fuller and more detailed manner precisely
what the unique sonship of Jesus meant to
the author of the Gospel. I shall seek to
show that what are sometimes called the
" inhistoricities " of his account have as the
clue to their just and right interpretation the
view I have already maintained as that which
is latent in the Synoptic portraiture—namely,
the consciousness of ethical and spiritual
solidarity possessed by Jesus. In other words,
I wish to show that the " historical " incom-

patibilities do not involve " real " incompatibility.

The real difference between the Synoptic portraiture and that of the Fourth Gospel is more one of *emphasis* than of *content*. And this difference of *emphasis* rests upon, such is my contention, two factors—one of which I will call the author's *chronological indifference*, the other of which I will call his *dramatising genius*. Both of these factors have their source in his whole rich and strong personality, the main key to which is his intuitional penetration to the real secret of Jesus.

This difference of emphasis is one that impresses every candid reader of the Gospel. The *total impression* which the Jesus of the Fourth Gospel makes upon him is that of one who, whatever else can be said of him, is Divine. The *total impression* which the Jesus of the Synoptists makes upon him is that of one who, whatever else he was, is a man. The teaching of Jesus in the Synoptic Gospels may be said to centre round the Kingdom ; the teaching of the Jesus in the Fourth Gospel may be said to centre round himself. In the first we find beautiful and illuminating parables, told in an objective manner ; in the second we have no one such parable, but discourses about his own status as the unique revealer of spiritual reality, illustrated by allegories told in a subjective manner. In these Johannine discourses Jesus from the beginning proclaims his unique filial and Messianic consciousness : it is placed in the very centre of the narrative from the first chapter. It is not just that it is *involved* in his words and deeds ; it is that it is announced and defended. John the Baptist, when he sees Jesus, immediately proclaims : " Behold the Lamb of God, which taketh away the sin of the world ! . . . And I have seen and have borne witness that this is the Son of God " (Jn. i. 29-34). Nathanael declares when he meets him, " Rabbi, thou art the Son of God ; thou art King of Israel " ; to which Jesus replies, " Verily, verily, I say unto you, Ye shall see the heaven opened, and the angels of God ascending and descending upon the Son of man " (Jn. i. 49-51), an announcement of the experienced fact, after-wards realised by the disciples, of the "ladder" which Jesus was to them, uniting the heavenly with the earthly, God with man. What is *implied* from the first in the Markan account is *explicitly avowed* from the first in the Johannine. When, later, the Jews openly ask for a plain avowal of his Messiahship he replies, " I told you, and ye did not believe," an answer revealing that to the writer that plain declaration had already been made (Jn. x. 24). In the Synoptic narrative, on the other hand, it would seem that it was not till Cæsarea Philippi that Jesus began to unveil to the disciples the deep secret of his conscious religious union with God. (I take the Lukan context for the "Q" utterance already discussed—Matt. xi. 25-7 ; Lk. x. 21-2—as the true historical context ; that is, it is *later* than the Confession at Cæsarea Philippi. Some have suggested that the occasion of the utterance may have been the Confession itself.) It is, indeed, coming to be felt by many modern students of the Gospels that Cæsarea Philippi represents an even more significant stage in the ministry of Jesus than had been recognised : it may mark not only a stage in his self-manifestation to his disciples, but a stage when his consciousness of the Father reaches its point of highest and all-comprehending intensity, bringing with it fuller light on the road which the Divine Will had marked out for him. However that may be—and we may well remember that this development is " his secret," which we can only ponder with a measure of deep and diffident reverence—the self-revelation, which in the Synoptists is made with a true teacher's educative and eliciting reserve, is made in the Johannine narrative with open and full declaratory avowal.

This difference of emphasis and of formal portraiture of Jesus is seen in the numerous " I am's " of the Fourth Gospel. In these sayings Jesus is represented as declaring in the first person singular that he *is* " the bread of life " (vi. 35, 48), " the light of the world " (viii. 12), " the door of the sheep," " the door " (x. 7, 9), " the good shepherd " (x. 11, 14), " the resurrection and the life " (xi. 25), " the way, the truth and the life "(xiv. 6), " the true vine," " the vine " (xv. 1, 5). Nowhere in the Synoptic Gospels do we find quite this type of utterance, where Jesus is held to claim *to be* what, indeed, he was to become to his followers. The nearest perhaps that we get to it is in his words spoken at the Last Supper, " this is my body " (Mk. xiv. 22 ; Matt. xxvi. 26 ; Lk. xxii. 19 ; 1 Cor. xi. 24), " this is my blood of the covenant " (Mk. xiv. 24 ; cp. Matt. xxvi. 28 ; Lk. xxii. 20 ; 1 Cor. xi. 25).

There remain two other Johannine passages to which there is no precise parallel in the Synoptists. In each Jesus is represented as definitely claiming pre-existence. " Before Abraham was, I am " (viii. 58) ; " And now, O Father, glorify thou me with thine own self with the glory which I had with thee before the world was " (xvii. 5). Nowhere in the Synoptic Gospels does Jesus make any claim for himself such as would involve, as these two passages seem to do, a memory of a " pre-existent," or perhaps we should say, " pre-temporal," state.

These differences, then, stand clear. How have they to be regarded ? I suggest that they may be naturally understood, and therefore rightly appreciated, in the light of the mind and whole personality of the author of the Gospel.

It should hardly be necessary to say in these historical days that an understanding of an author's mind is necessary to an understanding of an author's writings. Knowledge of a man helps us to understand why he said a certain thing in a certain way. It helps us also to understand his omissions, and his, sometimes exaggerated, sometimes warped, emphasis. Probably no one would have seen Johnson just as Boswell saw him. No great figure of history is ever limned twice with the same brush or the same colours. When we talk about our heroes we cannot but reveal ourselves. For we see in them what we have the capacity to see. There is a substratum of truth in the sceptical subjectivism of Anatole France when he says : " To be quite frank, the critic ought to say, ' Gentlemen, I am about to speak of myself à propos of Shakespeare, à propos of Racine, or of Pascal, or of Goethe.' " [1] Without acquiescing in the wholesale historical scepticism to which a one-sided emphasis on such subjectivity would lead us, I am convinced that if we do not remember this considera-

[1] In the Preface of *La Vie Littéraire*.

tion we shall not begin to understand the differences, in contrast with the Synoptic Gospels, presented to us by the Fourth Gospel. The Gospel portrays to us Jesus *in a Johannine setting.* It, therefore, reveals the author himself. And he is both seer and dramatist. The dramatist, unfortunately— as we are sometimes inclined to say—takes occasional control of the seer, instead of allowing himself always to be controlled by the seer. Most of us have known people who when they narrate an incident give a finer point to its moral by putting it, probably quite unconsciously, in a more dramatic setting than it possessed. In relating a conversation they will improve upon the words spoken in order to set forth a sharper antithesis. The author of the Fourth Gospel would have understood such people ; for they are of his own lineage. But in him there is a most penetrating spiritual insight and intuition added to this dramatic quality. He was, without doubt, an original genius.

The supreme difficulty which this Gospel has presented to exegetes all through the centuries arises, as I at least believe, from the fact that the writer is writing about the greatest religious figure of history, and that he himself has a combination of unique qualities of mind to which it is difficult to find a parallel. It is the conjunction of these two facts which creates the glory, and the perplexity, of this Gospel : these together create our difficulty, and together are the key to its solution. If only a Boswell had been writing about Jesus ! So we exclaim in certain moments when our perplexity is a mingling in fairly equal proportions of faithful desire and tired unimaginativeness. Happily for the abiding glory of the New Testament literature inspired by Jesus, we have many books by many writers ; and not the least glorious of these is the Gospel by an author who combined a penetrating spiritual insight into the mind of Jesus and a remarkable dramatic gift which took of the substance of history and wove it into a literary form of transcendent genius. After what I have said with regard to the sound Synoptic basis for the truth of this insight, it will not, I trust, be suggested that this theory is a mere guess. The theory is substantiated by two main facts which lie

open to every investigator : first, the fact
of the Synoptic Gospels, from which we see
that the Johannine portraiture is *qualitatively*,
if not quantitatively, right ; and second, the
fact of the Fourth Gospel, which bears on
the face of it marks of a characteristic transcendent genius.

It is this insight of the author which explains what I have called his chronological
indifference. Most germane to the position
here maintained is the indifference, already
discussed, to the time element in regard to
the self-manifestation of Jesus to his disciples.
Passing over the author's divergence from the
Synoptists with respect to the visits of Jesus
to Jerusalem and with respect to the date of
the Last Supper—on which it may be said
that the arguments are by no means all on
the side of the chronological accuracy of the
Synoptic narrative—we note that the incident
of the cleansing of the temple is placed in
the Fourth Gospel at the beginning of the
ministry. Here it is natural to suppose that
the Johannine evangelist, untroubled by the
scruples justly belonging to modern scientific
historians, places at the opening of his record

an incident which focusses at a very vivid point the unique ethical and spiritual consciousness of Jesus. The incident of the raising of Lazarus is not one which can be used to illustrate the writer's chronological indifference, inasmuch as the story is not found in the Synoptic record : rather, it illustrates the dramatic and allegorical character of his mind, with which, however, it is in the closest relationship. His unconcern for scientific accuracy shows itself sometimes in regard to precise dating, and sometimes in regard to the incidents themselves. And so the Lazarus story should probably be regarded as a free allegorising of some historical incident. I do not myself regard it as a " doctrinal allegory," for such a designation would suggest that there is more precise theologising in this Gospel than I should be inclined to admit, or than I am able to see. It is, rather, if I may venture the phrase, an " experiential allegory " ; that is, it is an allegory which endeavours to express both the deep, conscious experience of Jesus, and the experienced blessing of quickened life which his followers have received in his fellowship.

And the open clue to such an *experiential* interpretation is found in two utterances woven into the narrative : they are, first, the words of Jesus, " I am the Resurrection and the Life, he that believeth on me, though he were dead, yet shall he live ; and whosoever liveth and believeth on me shall never die " ; and, second, the reply of Martha, " I do believe that thou art the Christ, the Son of God, who was to come into the world " (Jn. xi. 25, 27). When he is called " Son of God " and " Christ " here, it is, I believe, to give expression to the *knowledge of God* possessed by Jesus and to the *consciousness of vocation* that flowed therefrom, not to a developed metaphysical Christology. And when upon his lips are put the words, " I am the Resurrection and the Life," it is, I believe, to give expression to the *whole* experience of quickening, mental, moral and spiritual, which his fellowship has brought, and not just to a theological or doctrinal interpretation which the Church came later to accept.

What it is supremely necessary to remember, when we read this Gospel is, first, that it is written by a man of transcendent genius, combining deep spiritual intuition with a sometimes overmastering — perhaps even occasionally distorting — dramatic faculty : and, second, that it is written about, and inspired by, the greatest religious figure of all time. It is, as I have said, the *combination* of these two facts which may so easily mystify our minds when we read his Gospel. Each of these factors, if it stood by itself, might well bewilder us. For Jesus is as much to-day, as in Matthew Arnold's day, " above our heads " ; and the Johannine author has a quality of mind very rare in Western countries—much more common in Eastern countries like India [1]—which, in spite of our best endeavours, leaves him something of an enigma. But when these two factors meet in one brief book ! That is, as I believe, the position that confronts us in the Johannine Gospel. It is as if we were asked to decide as we stand by the Rhone below Lyons

[1] I imagine that the least inadequate interpretation of this Gospel will come from an Indian Christian. Bishop Westcott, I have been told, used to say this. Candour compels me to add that some of my friends who have an intimate knowledge of India do not share this view.

which water is the Rhone's and which the Saône's. Little do we wonder that hundreds of interpretations, few of them in mutual accord, have poured from the press. Where is Jesus, and where is the author, we ask ourselves as we read this Gospel. How shall we disengage the two personal factors? How unravel so tangled a skein? When even the discourses of Jesus are continued by the author, and in the same style, so that we know not where discourse ends and comment begins, how can we hope to know either Jesus or the author?

I do not, I trust, overlook, or fail to face, these difficulties. Yet, there is one sure clue to guide us—namely, the unique religious consciousness of Jesus. This is, as I hold, the most sure historical fact about Jesus: it dominates the Synoptic narrative, to those who have eyes to see. And it is the writer's insight into this consciousness, expressed in ways characteristic of his genius, which gives us our second clue. The whole Gospel is controlled by his perception of the significance of Jesus.

THE GOSPEL NOT A DOGMATIC TREATISE, BUT HISTORY VIEWED *SUB SPECIE ÆTERNITATIS*.

It is, I feel, necessary to distinguish between a *dramatisation of doctrine* and a *dramatisation of that whole depth of the experience which gave rise to the doctrine*. If the writer is entitled to be called " theologos," it is not that he is in our modern sense a " theologian " ; nor, if his Gospel is entitled to be called, as it was by F. D. Maurice, " a perfect summary of Christian Theology," [1] is it that it is a coherent and systematic theology in our modern sense. (Perhaps I ought not to say " in our modern sense," for it seems to be a feature of modern theology that, in the present state of theological uncertainty, the ideal of a coherent system has for the moment been relinquished, the main endeavour being devoted to an understanding of the whole experience out of which theology sprang. In this respect we are, I believe, nearer to the environment of the Johannine author than any previous theological age.) The writer is a " theo-

[1] At p. 2 of his still valuable Commentary on the Johannine Gospel.

logian," in the sense that " pectus facit theo-
logum "—in the sense, that is, that *insight*
is the *prior* qualification to *reasoning*. His
Gospel is a " theology " not in the sense that
he is *inferring* theological propositions from
given data, but that he has penetrated to
the heart of his data and is seeking to let
these express themselves. And so I do not
think this writer is one who has convinced
himself that Jesus stood in a unique relation
to God, as an inference from the sublimity
of the Master's ethical teaching and life ;
I believe, rather, that by the spiritual quality
of his own mind he has been able to penetrate
with intuition to the immediacy of communion
which Jesus had with God. It is a mystic's
intuition of the certitude Jesus had of God,
a certitude which was the fount of his moral
insight and sublimity ; it was not an apologist's
" demonstration " of that certitude on the
basis of the outward facts. It is the insight which tells him that Jesus has union
with God *in sensu æternitatis ;* it is not the
inference which convinces him that Jesus has
union with God in a numerical, or physical,
or " metaphysical " sense. These inferences

came later ; the best minds of the Church were centred for generations on the endeavour to achieve them. Without under-estimating their task, we may, I think, agree that the task of the Johannine author was more fully and abidingly significant than theirs. More adequate interpretations may or may not be achieved by the Church—and all who have the faith and the hope and the incentive of the true theologian will not despair of the future in this respect ; but without the assurance that the temporal is bound to the eternal in the whole life and consciousness of Jesus, these can little avail. They will but evoke unhappy memories of certain " evidences " apologetic, which frequently seemed to seek a standing-ground for religion when essential religious faith itself had been lost or about which there was, at least, considerable latent dubiety. The mind of the Johannine author is far removed from that pugnacious argumentativeness which has not infrequently cloaked a deficiency in essential religion. " No one," he says, " has seen— [or, may we not add in fidelity to his thought, " proved "]—God at any time ; the only begotten Son who is in the bosom of the Father, he has made him known " (Jn. i. 18). And the " belief " in the Divine Son which he wishes to inspire in his readers through his record (xx. 31) is not the formal belief which rests upon " coercive proofs " ; it was the belief that Jesus was unique Son in the depth of his whole experience, which belief was to be seen in the new " life through his name."

His Gospel is neither " dogmatic treatise " nor yet " history with a dogmatic purpose " ; it is history viewed *sub specie æternitatis*, written in order to enkindle a similar apprehension.

This insight of the author, clothing itself in the dramatic and allegorical forms which came naturally to his mind, is manifest throughout the Gospel. It is seen in the symbolical value he seems to attach to numbers,[1] in the significant references to " water " and " blood," in the conflict between " light " and " darkness " which the presence of the Incarnate Word precipitates, and in the symbolism of the " miracles "

[1] See *The Fourth Gospel in Recent Criticism and Interpretation*, by Dr. W. F. Howard, pp. 184 and 271.

he chooses to relate. Whatever the historical nucleus behind these "miracles," their function in the narrative seems mainly to serve as texts from which to expound truths as to the Master's spiritual significance—the "new wine" of the Gospel which Jesus brings to renovate men's souls (see Jn. ii. 1-11), the spiritual sight which he, the Light of the World, brings to those conscious of their blindness (Jn. ix.), the "Resurrection and the Life" which Jesus is to those who have faith in him (see Jn. xi.).

There are, indeed, a few occasions in the Gospel when it would seem his dramatising bent of mind overleaps itself, and almost succeeds in stultifying his insight into the unique Divine consciousness of Jesus. Dramatic genius in an author, as I have already suggested, is always a peril : it may so easily distort the message it wishes to convey by false and unnatural accentuation. The peril is especially acute in such a case as this, where the author is dramatising a consciousness ; for whereas in the dramatisation of strictly historical events nothing suffers but the writer's dramatic

suffers, but the inner truth is there for those who will remember the situation. The reader of the Gospel will also note that the author himself corrects his " historical inaccuracy " on this issue. Nathanael is to Jesus " an Israelite indeed, in whom is no guile " (Jn. i. 47). Jesus, in his dialogue with the Samaritan woman, associates himself with the Jews and with the pure revelation which has come down through them : " *we* worship that which *we* know ; for salvation is of the Jews " (Jn. iv. 22). In this correction we have an interesting illustration of the common psychological fact that the inaccurately dramatic type of mind frequently contradicts itself by unconscious asides or spontaneous admissions. By such a type of mind these, from the strictly logical point of view, self-contradictions are seldom if ever perceived—to the interest or amusement of the listener or reader. Such minds are so possessed by their insight that for the moment the logical faculty is in abeyance, and they can see nothing else. So it was with the Johannine author. He is possessed by his insight into the significance of Jesus.

The same penetration is seen also in the

two pre-existence passages to which reference
has already been made. Just as in the "I
am" passages he very probably dramatises
his insight into Jesus's spiritual consciousness
and spiritual significance for mankind by
putting upon the lips of the Master words
which specifically claim all this, so in these
passages he gives to Jesus words which seem
explicitly to declare the non-temporal nature
of his true life in fellowship with the Father.
I dare not dogmatise here on what precise
words may have been spoken by Jesus in
regard to this issue. I find it myself wholly
congruous with the depth and continuity
of his fellowship with God to believe that on
different occasions, at least to his disciples,
he had sought to express to their somewhat
materialistic minds the reality of a life un-
bounded by the categories of time and space.
And understanding whatever words he spoke
in this sense—so perfectly harmonious with
the unfolding of his Sonship—I dare not
deny them a specific historical basis. Some
would make this non-temporal insight that
of the Johannine author ; it seems more
natural to me to regard it as the expressed

insight of Jesus himself, deeply apprehended
by our author during the years he spent with
"the beloved disciple"—whom I myself take
to be the apostle John. I regard these pre-
existence sayings, that is, to be not only the
interpretation of the "eternal" experiences of
the disciples of Jesus, but as involved in the
Master's own consciousness of God. In similar
manner, I understand all those passages which
speak of the complete dependence of Jesus
for " word " and for " work " upon the Father
(see Jn. viii. 28 ; xii. 44 ff. ; xiv. 24). Seen
in the light of the author's dominating purpose to reveal Jesus's conscious relation to
the Father, such utterances but express the
fruitful word and work made known in that
fellowship. " I do nothing of myself, but as
the Father taught me, I speak these things.
And he that sent me is with me ; he hath not
left me alone ; for I do always the things that
are pleasing to him." " The word which ye
hear is not mine, but the Father's who sent
me." In the fellowship of our human re-
lationships how much do we not " receive "
from our friends ? How much is " given "
to us by them—not just by outward direct

speech, but in the unseen and unheard fellowship of the spirit ! In the unique fellowship
which Jesus had with the Father, in the unique
obedience he rendered to His will, is it not
wholly fitting to suppose that he regarded
" all things " in his life as from above ?
It is for this reason, also, that he can fittingly
say that he that receiveth him, receiveth
Him that sent him (xiii. 20) ; and that, on
the other hand, he that hateth him, hateth
his Father also (xv. 23). His Father is
glorified when his disciples bring forth the
fruits of an obedient following of himself
(xv. 8). In all such sayings the kernel of
historical truth is his spiritual oneness with
the Father, which must have expressed itself
in manifold ways. And whatever precise
words were used by Jesus, it is only, as I
would think, spiritual blindness which would
regard them as expressive of a vainglorious
egotism. Jesus himself was conscious of our
creaturely limitations, as the Gospel clearly
reveals. Attachment to himself, therefore,
was not conceived by him in any self-centred
manner. It was not attachment to him
in sensu humanitatis, but *in sensu æternitatis* :

it was attachment to the revelation of the Divine and Eternal of which he knew, in his ethical and spiritual consciousness, he was the medium.

THE *LOGOS* PROLOGUE.

It is this spiritual insight of the author, further, into the spiritual consciousness and spiritual significance of Jesus which should guide us in interpreting the much-disputed *Logos* Prologue. A flood of scholarly discussion has poured forth from the press during the past generation upon this term *Logos* and what it implies. The question has with erudite research been explored as to the precise *derivation* of the concept. Is it Hebraic or Hellenistic ? Are we to look for its ancestry in the " Memra," or " Word," of the Lord in the Targums, or in the Old Testament, or in Philo, or in contemporary Stoicism, or in the Mystery and Hermetic literature ? The *real* value, I take it, of such investigation is that it should assist us in deciding the precise connotation given to the term by the author of the Fourth Gospel. And I would suggest that what the word meant to the author can best be determined by its use in his own context. What matters is not the term, but the idea conveyed by the term. The same words mean different things as used by different minds. Of words it might be said : The Form remains, the Content ever changes. The " ancestry " of an " idea " has no doubt a certain importance ; such investigation should, for example, help us to remember that the whole past of humanity is the womb of every idea held by our modern minds. The womb of an idea, however, is not the idea itself. Each notion held by a modern man has its " ancestry," but the notion itself is *his own*, having gained its unique identity within the depths of his own personal consciousness. There are, I believe, certain people who are permitted to undertake painstaking researches in the archives of Somerset House in order to trace the lineage of living men, with their thoughts, emotions and wills. But the lineage of the physical, mental, moral and spiritual characteristics of a man is not the man himself. He has *his own* body, *his own* mind, *his own* moral and spiritual nature. My main in-

.terest here is not lineage, but the living man
—what he thinks, what he says, what he does.
I wish, therefore, to stress that the content
of an idea is not its mould.

If this method of approach to the interpretation of the *Logos* in the mind of our author
is right, we shall see that the Prologue is to
be read in the light of his " meaning " in the
Gospel as a whole. (I take it that the Prologue is indissolubly one with the rest of the
Gospel. Theories of " partition " which would
sever it from the main narrative seem to me
to be dictated by a false reading of the *Logos*
and its place in the Gospel.) And, once
again, it is as we remember the dramatic
and allegorical character of his mind penetrating to, and seeking to unfold, the unique
filial consciousness of Jesus that we shall
see what he meant to say in this Prologue.

It is his insight which sees that Jesus is
God's " Word " ; it is his dramatic symbolism which declares that this " Word " is
eternally " with God," and is eternally
" Divine " (i. 1—ἦν πρὸς τὸν θεόν, καὶ θεὸς ἦν
ὁ λόγος).

As a true mystic—if I may use a word of

ambiguous connotation to describe him—he believed that God *spoke* within the depths of a man's consciousness. What was this " word " in our inner life but the *purpose* and *activity* of God ? For what indeed is any " word " but the expression of thought, emotion and volition ? And from being the *expression*, the " word " comes to designate *the thought, the emotion, and the volition itself.* Thus God's " Word " within the soul becomes *His very Presence* within the soul. Every true mystic speaks in this way, whether he be or be not an " ontological " mystic. So, for example, Wordsworth speaks of " conscience " as " God's most intimate presence in the Soul " ; and the unmystical Shakespeare speaks of " conscience " as " this Deity in my bosom." The writer of the Fourth Gospel had a heritage of similar ideas in his own, as I believe, Hebrew nation. The " Word of God " which came to the prophets was the very thought and purpose of God, as known within their own conscious life. The Hebrew mind regarded the personal life as *a unity*, and so was unable to acquiesce in the false psychology which severs a man's thought

from his emotion or from his will. For
that reason God's " Word " was to them His
very " activity." His " Word " was creative
action both within the soul and without in
the universe as a whole. Thus we read in
the first chapter of Genesis, " God *said*,
Let there be light ; and there was light."
A similar mode of expression is found in the
Psalms. In Psalm xxxiii. verse 6, for example,
we read, " *By the word of Yahveh* were the
heavens made, and all their host by the breath
of his mouth." Or again, " The nations
raged, the kingdoms were moved ; *He uttered
His voice*, the earth melted. The Lord of
hosts is with us ; the God of Jacob is our
refuge " (Ps. xlvi. 6-7). Is it not significant
for the thought of the Psalmist that the
" presence " of " the Lord of hosts " is manifest in the " uttering of His voice " which
"melts the earth "? (see also such passages as
Ps. cxlvii. 18, and Ps. cxlviii. 8). The same
thought is found in the Wisdom literature
of the Old Testament, where the Divine
" Wisdom " is regarded as the activity of
the whole mind of God. When God " established the heavens, I was there. . . . When

He marked out the foundations of the earth,
Then I was by him, as a master-workman "
(Prov. viii. 27-30). In the Wisdom of Solomon
it is said of " wisdom " that " she is a breath
of the power of God, And a clear effluence of
the glory of the Almighty " (vii. 25). In the
same chapter the writer continues : " For
she is an effulgence from everlasting light,
And an unspotted mirror of the working of
God, And an image of His goodness. And
she, being one, hath power to do all things ;
And remaining in herself, reneweth all things ;
And from generation to generation passing
into holy souls She maketh men friends of
God and prophets. . . . For to the light of
day succeedeth night, But against wisdom
evil doth not prevail " (Wis. vii. 26-30).
(Many of these expressions recall New Testament expressions—the last verse quoted,
for example, reminding us forcibly of the
Johannine author's statement that " the light
shineth in the darkness, and the darkness did
not overcome it.") In the book of Ecclesiasticus many significant attributes are ascribed
to " wisdom," and the famous words of in-
vitation in Matt. xi. 28-30 may have been

influenced by the passage in Ecclesiasticus
li. 23 ff.

As I have already indicated my main interest here is not in tracing the kinship of
the Johannine author's ideas with those of
the intellectual and spiritual environment
of his time. Nevertheless, it is significant
that in the literature of his own nation, when
the thought and activity of God were held
to be present, such terms as " word " and
" wisdom " should be employed. Now, this
writer's supreme message is his insight into
the inner consciousness of Jesus wherein, as
Jesus himself knew, God was present in thought
and emotion and act. Deep there, Jesus
knew the Father's mind, quickened to the
Father's love—" for Thou lovedst me before
the foundation of the world," xvii. 24—was
assured that he was the vehicle of the Father's
activity. Into this spiritual consciousness the
Johannine writer had a profound insight.
When, therefore, he sought to express his
central thesis in the prologue how more
fittingly and naturally—and, may I add,
sublimely—than in the famous verses before
us. From all eternity there has been the

omnipresent thought and activity of God :
" In the beginning was the Word, and the
Word was with God, and the Word was
Divine." All that is has come to be through
this Divine thought and activity : " All
things were made by him, and without him
was not anything made that hath been made."
Life itself had its source in this Divine thought
and activity, and this Divinely-originated life
has been the illumination of men : " In him
was life and the life was the light of men."
Amid the darkness of sinful mortality the
Light has ever shone, and has never been
overcome. And so this Divine thought and
activity, this essential Divine Presence, came
to dwell in the mortal Jesus we knew ; and
as we looked upon him we saw the Glory of
the very Divine Presence ; and if we would
describe this Glory, so full of grace and truth,
how more fittingly than to say that it was the
Glory of one who knew himself to be as the
only son of his father. So uniquely did the
Divine Presence dwell within him, so intimate
and so trustful was this fellowship—like that,
again, between a father and his only son—
that though no one has ever seen God, yet as

we read his life and pondered upon its secret we said, surely God is here in very Presence.

I have sought to paraphrase the salient words of the Prologue, in order to show their coherence with the suggestion I have made, namely, that the dominating thought of the writer is the unique knowledge of God possessed by Jesus. It is this conscious fellowship which is itself the " incarnation " of the " Word." It is not that the Divine thought and activity comes to repose like a static substance upon another substance. It is not that the Divine mind stands side by side with a human mind, and that in this vehicle of two types of mind there is a continual drama as of two actors playing on the same stage at the same time. It is not that here in this Jesus there is a combination of two alternating activities—the Divine and the human. It is that this Fellowship with God in the undivided mind of Jesus *is* the Divine thought. It is that this harmony of the will of Jesus with God, this obedience in his whole conscious life to God, *is* the Divine activity.

Such an interpretation of the Logos Prologue, it will be seen, makes it harmonious with the whole Gospel, and not, as it has been commonly regarded, a kind of detached philosophical prelude. The historic Jesus is God's "Word" in time and place. The key to the Gospel is the religious consciousness of Jesus ; and the same key opens to us what has been so often thought to be the mysterious door of the Prologue. The Prologue, I believe, is only a mystery to those who approach it with philosophical, or, I would rather say, metaphysical, presuppositions. Interpreting it in the light of the Philonic Logos Divine Principle which mediates between the Transcendent God and the natural universe, these regard it as having little more relation to the rest of the Gospel than a philosophical introduction has to a dogmatic treatise. Harnack, it will be remembered, regarded the Prologue in this way ; and I find that most ministers and students of the Christian religion to-day are inclined to acquiesce in this view. Harnack expressed his judgement thus : " The Prologue of the Gospel is not the key to its comprehension. It begins with a well-known great object, the Logos, re-adapts and transforms it —implicitly opposing false Christologies—in

order to substitute for it Jesus Christ, the
μονογενὴς θεός, in order to unveil it as this
Jesus Christ. The idea of the Logos is allowed
to fall from the moment that this takes place.
The author continues to narrate of Jesus only
with the view of establishing the belief that
he is the Messiah, the Son of God." He says
later : " As nowadays a section on the nature
of the Christian religion is usually prefixed
to a treatise on dogmatics, in order to pre-
pare and introduce the reader, so also the
Johannine prologue seems to be intended as
an introduction of this kind. It brings in
conceptions which were familiar to the Greeks,
in fact it enters into these more deeply than
is justified by the presentation which follows ;
for the notion of the Incarnate Logos is by
no means the dominant one here." [1]

I believe, on the contrary, that the Prologue *is* the key to the comprehension of the
whole Gospel. But it can only be seen to be
such if the " Word " is interpreted as the
experienced thought and activity of God.
This it was to many Hebrew minds, as represented by the Old Testament. And what

[1] *History of Dogma*, E.T., vol. i., pp. 97 and 329.

the Johannine writer is saying is that this Divine thought and activity has been uniquely seen in the historic Jesus. So conceived, the thought of the Divine "Word" runs through the whole Gospel. The author says on every page that Jesus is the expressed mind and purpose of God. This creative thought of God has been operative through all the ages, and is now uniquely manifest in Jesus. The very word *logos* is frequently used in the later chapters of the Gospel, and it is only because the Logos of the Prologue has been metaphysically interpreted that these later uses of the word have been thought to have no kinship with it. Once it is seen that the "Word" is the experienced religious manifestation of God, the later references of Jesus in the Gospel to his "word" fall at once into complete harmony with the whole context. "He that heareth my *word*," says Jesus, "and believeth Him that sent me hath eternal life, and cometh not into judgement, but hath passed out of death into life" (v. 24). To hear the word of Jesus, in this context, is to come into fellowship with the whole mind of Jesus—a mind which reveals the Creative thought of God. " If ye abide in my *word*," says Jesus to the Jews who had believed him, "then are ye truly my disciples" (viii. 31). Again the thought is that if they remain in harmonious accord with the mind and purpose of Jesus, they will be his disciples—and the mind and purpose of Jesus is the expression of the mind and purpose of God. So also are to be interpreted all such other passages as : " ye have not His (God's) *word* abiding in you : for whom He sent, him ye believe not " (v. 38) ; " ye seek to kill me because my *word* hath not free course in you " (viii. 37) ; " Why do ye not understand my speech ? because ye cannot hear my *word* (viii. 43) ; "now ye are clean through the *word* which I have spoken unto you " (xv. 3) ; "I have given them Thy *word*" (xvii. 14) ; " Thy *word* is truth " (xvii. 17). These, and many other passages throughout the Gospel, fall into harmonious accord with the Logos Prologue as I have here interpreted it.

Further, it is only because the Johannine Logos Prologue has been philosophically, or metaphysically, conceived that interpreters

have failed to note parallel uses in the
rest of the New Testament. The Johannine
author is not the only New Testament
writer who speaks of Jesus as " Logos."
The author of the Apocalypse—whom I do
not take to be the Johannine author—calls
Jesus " the *logos* of God " (Rev. xix. 13).
The author of the epistle to the *Hebrews*
says that " the *logos* of God is living and
active, and sharper than any two-edged
sword, and piercing even to the dividing of
soul and spirit, of both joints and marrow,
and quick to discern the thoughts and intents
of the heart. And there is no creature that
is not manifest in his sight " (iv, 12). Luke,
in the introduction to his Gospel, speaks of
those who were " eyewitnesses and ministers
of the *logos*," where it is at least conceivable
to suppose that the genitive is connected with
" eyewitnesses " as well as with " witnesses "
—and in this case the reference would be
to Jesus, the Divine *Logos*.

I believe, further, that the *abruptness* with
which the author launches his theme in the
first verse of the Prologue is entirely con-
sonant with this experiential interpretation

of the *Logos*. It is the abruptness of an overmastering insight. The author has not the temperament of the metaphysician, who moves slowly but surely to his conclusions. There is a dogmatic quality in the author's beginning—" In the beginning was the *Logos*, and the *Logos* was with God, and the *Logos* was Divine." It is not, however, the dogmatic quality which characterises the dogmatic theologian : it is the dogmatic quality which reveals the intuitive seer. He does not, like the philosopher—or, I should say, like some philosophers—seek to convince himself, and others, that he is the seeker, and not the dogmatist. He knows that he is not the seeker, for he has seen, he has found. And he says so with the abruptness of settled conviction. He is not arguing, he is stating : he is not reasoning, he is declaring. His conclusion comes at the beginning, for it is a " conclusion " which is the beginning, middle and end of the whole Gospel. He writes, not to convince by the cogent sequence of his arguments, but by the illuminating nature of his all-controlling insight. Here in the opening sentences of his Gospel there is no studied, philosophic caution : there is, instead, the direct and unstudied abandon of the seer.

I take the Prologue, therefore, as what I may call an *experiential* Prologue, not as a *metaphysical* Prologue. The Church has built a metaphysic upon this experiential basis ; but, I would say again, this metaphysic is not itself that basis. Often it has been said that the substance of the later dogmatic Christology is already present in the Prologue to this Gospel. What I wish to suggest is that *it was not so to the writer*. The Church has sought to interpret this Prologue, with all the other data of the New Testament, in a rational, coherent setting ; it has sought to elucidate what may be called the " metaphysical implications " of this Prologue. But that is not the same thing as saying that the Prologue contains the substance of dogmatic Christology. The whole *milieu* is different. The one is religion ; the other is theology. The one is Faith ; the other is Belief. The one is Foundation ; the other is Superstructure. And in saying these things, I do not say that theology is unnecessary to

religion, that Faith can dispense with Belief,
or that no Super-structure need be built on
the sure Foundation. Nevertheless, the dis-
tinction must be made. And so, for example,
the writer did not *himself* express in verse 3
of the Prologue the dogma of " the Cosmic
Christ." Nor did *he himself* express in verse
14 the dogma of the Incarnation. These
dogmas, however legitimate and, to the frailty
of our finite mortality, necessary they may
seem to our minds, came later, in response
to another kind of impulsion than that which
the Johannine author himself knew. For the
author, this Logos Prologue does not, I believe, express a theological speculation : it
expresses the religious insight and conviction that the Eternal, Creative, Ever-Active,
Ever-Illuminative, Word of God had been
uniquely manifested in the historic figure of
Jesus Christ. It is no doctrinal and speculative innovation that he here declares. This
is no *new* truth to the Church. The author
is but expressing *in a unique way* a truth that
has been central from the beginning to the
Christian community. He does not, as I
understand his meaning, begin his Gospel

with a theory of the Person of Christ. He begins with an insight into his Person. He does not move from a speculative metaphysic of Christ's relation to God and to the created universe to the historic deeds and the historic teaching. He moves from the essential fact of the consciousness and vocation of Jesus to a dramatic unfolding of that consciousness and sense of vocation in word and deed.

I am, therefore, compelled to dissent from the view of Dr. E. F. Scott, who holds that " the main fact " of the Logos Prologue is that the author " rests his account of the Christian revelation on a speculative idea, borrowed, with whatever differences, from Philo." I believe, on the contrary, that the author is expressing a religious insight into the essential religious significance of Jesus, and that *in his own mind* there is little or nothing in common with Hellenic or Hellenistic speculative ideas. I do not believe, as Dr. Scott believes, that a " judgement of faith " is, *in the author's own mind*, stated " in terms of an arbitrary theological idea." [1]

[1] *The Fourth Gospel, its Purpose and Theology* (1926 edition, pp. 160 and 162).

I believe, on the contrary, that it is his
ancient and modern interpreters who have
read this " arbitrary theological idea " into
the author's mind. The fact that the ancient
interpreters for the most part acquiesced in
this speculative, theological idea, while the
modern interpreters for the most part reject,
or at least maintain the inadequacy of, it
does not for the moment concern me. For
at this stage I am seeking to expound what
the *author himself* meant, and not what we
can make of what he meant.

Nor do I think, to use the words of Dr.
H. R. Mackintosh, that the author seeks
to offer " an articulated view of the relationship of Christ to God, when followed up into
its final implications." [1] What he seeks to
offer, as I understand his mind, is *the secret of
Jesus*, a secret which is of a deeper order of
reality than an articulated view of the relation of his Person to God. And the " final
implications " which concerned him were not
the speculative philosophical or theological
implications, but the practical and experiential
spiritual and ethical implications.

[1] *The Person of Jesus Christ* (1920 edition, p. 96).

SUMMARY OF CONCLUSIONS.

Let me now try to sum up what I have sought to maintain was the author's *Meaning* in this Gospel.

1. *It is penetrating insight into the filial consciousness of Jesus.*—This is the real historical basis of the Gospel. This is the main clue to the author's meaning. It is, therefore, not exact scientific history. The lines in *The Prelude* in which Wordsworth spoke of his experiences at Cambridge seem, with a measure of fitness, to adumbrate the perplexities of this " historical " issue :

I cannot say what portion is in truth
The naked recollection of that time,
And what may rather have been called to
   life
By after-meditation.

There is, I have suggested, a certain amount of direct personal " recollection," dating back to early days in Jerusalem when he was brought near to the " Jesus of History." There was much more indirect or mediated " recollection," gained through long communing with " the beloved disciple." Both

in the former direct " recollection " and in
the latter mediated " recollection," however,
there was intermingled much profound "after-
meditation." But this " after-meditation "
was centred on the objective reality of the
Master's unique fellowship in thought and
deed with God.

The Johannine author ante-dated by over
eighteen centuries some of our modern " psychological " historians. He believed that the
" truest " and least inadequate " history "
of any man is not just an exact record of
events and sayings ; that it involves *insight*
into the personality portrayed. The author
does not just explore the surfaces of things :
he would treat of Jesus as he is in himself.
While a work which is scientifically historical
must be in the scientific sense true ; yet a
work may be *essentially* true without being
scientifically historical. If I may use the
Gospel's own words in this context, " it is
the spirit that quickeneth." And this life-
giving insight impels the author to *choose*
what seems to him to reveal most clearly
the inner secret of his hero. The Johannine
evangelist himself tells us in chapter xx.,

7

verses 30-31, that this was his method and intention in writing. What is supremely necessary in a true historian is a quickening *rapport* between himself and the subject of his record. This, I have maintained, existed between the mind of Jesus and the Johannine author. He is, if I may apply to him Walt Whitman's words, a " Chanter of Personality " —a chanter of the Personality of Jesus. And he sang so well because he was, if I may use the phrase, of the spiritual lineage of Jesus. It would take a Jesus fully to understand Jesus—

Only themselves understand themselves and
the like of themselves,
As souls only understand souls—

but the New Testament writer nearest to the soul of Jesus is, I believe, the author of the Fourth Gospel.

2. *It is the dramatised essence of Christian theology.*—It is not formal theology itself ; it is the experiential basis of it. Here, as in the former paragraph, I have to steer a straight course between a Scylla and Charybdis—a course which I am convinced is the just historical course. Where, in the preceding issue,

Scylla was *complete inhistoricity* and Charybdis was *exact historicity*, so here Scylla is *precise theology* and Charybdis is *false theology*. The basis of all theology is experience, but theology itself is not precisely that experience. It is for this reason that this Gospel, concerned as it is primarily with the experience of Jesus, and secondarily with the experience of his disciples in his abiding fellowship, is neither formal theology nor a false basis for such a theology. For these very reasons it has the soundest of all bases for a true Christian theology. This being so, I find it impossible to acquiesce in the judgement on this Gospel of the late Dr. Bernard Bosanquet. " In one sense," he said, " it brings insight into the spirit of Christ to its highest perfection ; in another sense it begins the degeneration of spiritual religion into theological super-stition." [1] For, in the first place, if what Bosanquet called " theological superstition " *began from* this Gospel it did not, as I under-stand its meaning, *begin* there. Understood in the light of the author's own meaning, the Gospel is not itself speculation on theological

[1] In *Essays and Addresses*, p. 154.

and metaphysical issues—speculation which must ever be inadequate to Reality ; it is the glowing centre of religion itself. And, in the second place, the Church's endeavours to interpret or explicate in rational terms this essential core of her religion will not be regarded as mere " theological superstition," except by those who have a false and mistaken view of the function for which theology was created. It was not meant to take the place of religion. Its function is to interpret in terms of reason that which is supra-rational. Often, alas, the Church's own teachers have given a primary, instead of a secondary, place and function to theology ; and for this reason their efforts after theological system have not unjustly been called " theological superstitions." Theology is always " superstition " when it regards its statements as final, or its function as absolute. But theology in itself is no more superstition because of the " superstitious " views of some theologians, than science is superstition because some scientists hold the " superstitious " view that scientific theories are final explanations of Reality. And what I am here maintaining is that in so far as some of the Church's theologians regarded the function of theology in a " superstitious," or absolute, manner, they were departing from the essential insight of the author of the Fourth Gospel.

A great deal of what we call " Christology " represents the endeavour to put a living spirit into the strait jacket of metaphysical formulas, with the result that the spirit has been killed, or at least imprisoned. Our great trouble is that, by the very constitution of our minds, we *have* to express in formulas a reality which, by its very nature, *cannot* be so expressed. We *have* to do so, further, because of the pedagogic function of the Church ; we are called to make Christianity's children understand, and they " understand " by doctrinal formulas. Yet in " understanding " by formulas we may lose the vital reality.

The only escape from this dilemma of our finite mortality is by recognising the *provisional* nature of all our formulas. We shall then allow each successive age freedom to achieve new, better, or less inadequate statements. But the indispensable condition for the achievement of such new statements is a penetrating insight into the spiritual reality that was in Christ. This insight must inspire, dominate and control all such Christological endeavours—otherwise our last state will be worse than the first.

Theology divorced from religious insight is not of the lineage of the Johannine author. It was, as I have said, his religious insight, expressed through the medium of a dramatising faculty of rare genius, that gave birth to his Gospel, which is thus, through and through, dramatic. This colour, which shines through the whole canvas, is, I believe, the distilled essence of his " inborn aptitudes " fused by his long meditations on the mind of Jesus. Here we have a Gospel which is the fruit of a deep and original mind that has been long at work, both consciously and subconsciously, upon the inner truth about Jesus. Those who have watched the processes of their own minds will see how the whole record is thus illumined. When we dwell long upon striking historical incidents, or upon some outstanding personality, allowing " the subconscious mind " to ruminate upon them,

they take on an incisiveness, a clarity, a
dramatic colour which in the resultant narrative or portraiture throws into relief the
significant and into shadow the peripheral.
I know no finer illustration of this than the
Fourth Gospel :

" *And so the Word became flesh and stayed*
    among us ;
and we saw his glory—such a glory as is
    seen in one
who is the only son of his father—
full of grace and truth."

CHAPTER 11

THE MESSAGE

IN discussing the " meaning " of the
Fourth Gospel as it existed in the
author's own mind, I have almost necessarily
indicated some features of what I regard as
its abiding " message." In accordance with
the principle that no one can seek to interpret another's mind without in a measure
revealing his own, this I am free frankly to
acknowledge. In our modern writing on
the great issues of religion and theology the
personal standpoint of the writer may be
concealed—by, for example, an " objective "
presentation which scrupulously avoids the
use of the first personal pronoun. Nevertheless, to those who have eyes to see, the
" subjective " factor is always latent in the
" objective " discussion, and in the case of
an investigation of so intrinsically " interior "
a book as this Gospel this factor can be read
by those who run. In these days when so

much is subject to reconsideration and re-interpretation no *apologia* should be needed for a use of such phrases as " so it seems to me," " as I think," " such is my judgement." The avoidance of such confessional avowals, indeed, might suggest a " dogmatic " stand-point on the part of the writer to questions about which, both in point of fact and almost from the nature of the case, there is consider-able diversity of interpretation. The " true humility " of which Tennyson spoke is not always manifest in those who avoid the first personal pronoun on debatable issues.

Nevertheless, though the " message " has been adumbrated, there is need to endeavour to limn it in clearer outlines against the back-ground of some modern pertinent questions in dispute. The world moves on in thought and endeavour, and each new generation adds to the whole cultural environment of an age. Thus it is that an author's " mean-ing," however " true " it is, has to be re-lated to an environment which was not precisely his.

> " *All flows, and even the old are rapidly*
>   *flowing away,*
> *And the young are flowing in the throes of*
>   *a great alteration.*" [1]

It is for " the young " to see that " in the throes " of inevitable alteration the new body will be indwelt by the vital insights of the past.

[1] D. H. Lawrence.

(I) *The Gospel of God and the Historic Jesus.*
—During the nineteenth century, when so
many of the dogmatic systems of the past
were being slowly but surely undermined
by new thoughts which were burrowing deep
into the sub-conscious mind of the age, it
was frequently suggested that the Church
was entering upon a kind of Johannine dis-
pensation. Some even divided the whole
era of Christianity into three periods : the
Petrine, prior to the Reformation ; the Pauline,
subsequent to the Reformation ; and the
Johannine, the period just then beginning.
No just thinker would regard such a generalisa-
tion as wholly true. Nevertheless, it is suggestive, and has at least this measure of truth
in it, as far as our modern period is concerned,
that we to-day are peculiarly in a position
to appreciate the Johannine writer's insight,
and, therefore, peculiarly in a position to
assimilate it to our own experience. And
by that I mean that *our own age has many
points of resemblance to that to which the
Johannine author spoke with such satisfying
penetration and illumination.*

The main resemblance to which I wish to draw attention is in regard to the person of Jesus. The age to which the Johannine author spoke in the nineties of the first century was one which, we must suppose—as far, that is, as the thinking Christian minds were concerned—had assimilated the main historic facts of the life of Jesus as presented in the Synoptic Gospels. Those Gospels had been written for a generation which was, I imagine, in need of the *historic* emphasis which they supplied. The tradition as to the life and teaching of the Jesus of history had been precariously dependent, during the generation subsequent to the crucifixion, upon the oral transmission of a comparatively few first- and second-hand witnesses, and upon some incidental written accounts of the Master's sayings and deeds (cp. Lk. i. 1 and such documents as the *Logia*, which doubtless Matthew used but which cannot be precisely dated). With the Church scattered as it was through the Empire, there existed towards the end of this generation, as I cannot but think, a real danger that the historic Jesus should fade into a half-

forgotten past from which she was travelling
further and further away. This danger may
probably have been intensified owing to the
fact that the apostle responsible for the
founding of so many of these scattered churches
was Paul. He, while tenacious of a few fundamental facts of the earthly life of Jesus,
was, almost necessarily, chiefly concerned with
a message about the heavenly Christ. He had
few, if any, personal memories of the Jesus
of history : [1] and the outstanding Christian
fact of his life was his experience of the risen
Christ on the Damascus road. These two
factors, the one negative and the other
positive, would by a psychological necessity
determine his main emphasis. And that this
is so can be seen from his extant epistles—
and I say this, while remembering the
exceeding value of the contribution he made.
The writing of our Synoptic Gospels must
have corrected that danger, for these must
very speedily have been circulated in a
half-official way throughout the Church's

---

[1] The 2 Cor. v. 16 passage has been frequently interpreted as indicating that Paul had seen Jesus in the flesh,
and, as frequently, this interpretation has been rejected.

far-flung territories. But the assimilation of the historic emphasis of these Gospels must have itself created its own perplexities, and so brought in its train a new danger. The perplexities would arise through the endeavour to relate in thought the Jesus of history, with *his own* faith and *his own* teaching, to the Christ of Paul's gospel, with a faith *centred on him* as its objective basis. Arising out of these perplexities there sprang the Gnostic and Docetic endeavour to negate the value of the historical in the interests of a speculative mysticism. This Gnostic stream had begun to trickle towards the close of the first century, and was in full flow in the second century. An indication of this Docetic peril is seen in the Colossian epistle and in the two Johannine epistles. Already it had been necessary to counter " the Colossian heresy " with the emphasis that in Christ " are all the treasures of wisdom and knowledge hidden," and that " in him dwelleth all the fulness of the Godhead bodily "—σωματικῶς, with a bodily manifestation (Col. ii. 3 and 9). This incipient or rudimentary Gnosticism which had appeared in the later years of Paul's life had

been developing since his death. There were
now those who were proclaiming throughout the Christian world that Jesus Christ
was not come in the flesh (see 1 Jn. iv. 3 ;
2 Jn. 7).

It was to such an age, confronted with such
perplexities, and with so specific a danger,
that the Johannine author wrote, with an
emphasis which was at one and the same time
centred on the historic Jesus and oriented
to the eternity of God. By penetrating to
the eternal *in* that consciousness he lifted
it above the realm of the merely historical.
By the insight of a *faith* which had come to
him through meditation on the *faith* of
Jesus he was able to see, and to portray, the
Divine in the human, the abiding in the
transitory. And so instead of negativing
the *historical* in the interests of a Gospel *of
God*, the historic facts themselves became
the medium of God's very Word. Instead
of cutting off the temporal from the eternal,
the temporal became the manifestation of
the eternal. The teaching of a human Jesus,
speaking in a human voice and in a human
language, became the teaching of the Word,

speaking in a Divine voice and in the language of the heavenlies. The Eternal Word had become flesh in the person of Jesus, and had dwelt among men, so that his " glory " had been seen by them (Jn. i. 18). Such was the author's emphatic assertion in his Gospel, an assertion which is both historical and eternal. With a similar declaration, the same author begins his first epistle : " That which was from the beginning, that which we heard, that which we saw with our eyes, that which we beheld, and our hands touched, concerning the Word of life (the life was manifested, and we saw it, and we bear witness, and we declare to you that eternal life which was with the Father, and was manifested to us) : that which we saw and heard we declare to you " (1 Jn. i. 1-3).

In both these prologues there is the unswerving assertion that in a definite historical figure Eternity had been made known, God had been revealed. It is as if the author would tell us that the harmonies we are to hear in and through the pages that follow are not original but derived, they have their source in the unique consciousness and activity of the historic Jesus ; and, further, that the harmonies of that unequalled life flowed from Eternity. They are thus neither the imaginative nor speculative creation of the Johannine author : they are, if I may use the word, a *transmission*—a transmission from Eternity into Time, from God to the Man Christ Jesus, and through him to the author himself. At the present moment as I write, I hear the majestic strains of Beethoven's Eroica Symphony, transmitted from London to an adjoining room of my house. Let this be regarded as an illustration of what I mean when I say that the harmonies of this Gospel have had elsewhere their originating reality. The music I hear has been *transmitted ;* it is a reproduction of a reality existent in the Queen's Hall, London. It is not, if I may use the illustration of a recent German invention, what may be called " Synthetic music." In this, musical " records " have been produced, closely resembling those associated with the normal film, without these sounds ever having existed. The " composer " draws them with ink and brush ; they are then turned into sound by the use of

8

an ordinary film-projecting apparatus. Thus, in " synthetic music " we get *original* sound, not derived or transmitted sound. (In passing, I may say that certain views of the composition and nature of the Fourth Gospel, bring it into line with this " synthetic music." To such views the Gospel is an *original* speculative creation of the author—" original," not in the sense that it manifests the unique quality of the author's mind, but in the sense that it is in essence a theology created and fashioned on the slenderest historical basis by the author's mind.) In the Fourth Gospel, to my own view, the harmonies we hear are, as the author himself declares in his prologue, a transmitted expression of a reality existent in the life of the historic Jesus : and this historical reality is a transmitted expression of the Reality of God.

The resemblance of the Johannine situation to that of our own day seems to my own mind to be striking. For, in the first place, it may be said that the last two generations have recovered for us the historical Jesus, probably as well as he may be recovered. On some points there is still obscurity, but the main

outlines stand clear. It can hardly be denied
that until the intensive historical inquiry of
these recent decades Jesus, as he was in the
days of his flesh, had been for long ages, if
not wholly lost sight of, at least very much
obscured behind the affirmations of Christological Dogma. Speculative constructions had
almost blotted out the historical figure. A
dark trinitarian transaction had almost concealed the earthly ministry. The abstractions
of Soteriology had almost made men forget
the realities of the saving truths Jesus taught
and the saving obedience he demanded.
Beginning from a misreading of the Johannine author's *religious* teaching about the
" Eternal Word," the Church had come to
define the essential Being of God in terms of
a *Logos* doctrine, metaphysically conceived.
Reminders such as Augustine's that the
real meaning of the Trinitarian Dogma was
the exclusion of error rather than the in-
clusion of the whole absolute truth about God
—witness, for example, his famous passage
in *De Trinitate*, where he says : " three
persons, not that it might be spoken, but lest

it be left unspoken " (*ne taceretur*) [1]—were occasional and hardly represented the *real* teaching of the Church. If in treatises, read only by the learned, the negative and provisional nature of such a Dogma was recognised, in the Athanasian Creed, authoritatively promulgated and publicly recited, the positive and absolute nature of the Dogma was enforced by the direst anathemas. Can it then be wondered at that men everywhere came to think that the Church's theologians had construed the Being of God "satisfactorily" for all subsequent ages ? " The present distress " in theology has arisen largely because of the notion of the absoluteness and finality of such credal statements as taught by the Church.

Into all the causes for this obscuration of the Jesus of history I dare not here fully enter, interesting and significant though the question is. It is not sufficient to say that Christological Dogma was the " cause " of this concealment. The question goes deeper than that, and leads to the *psychological motivations* and *philosophical principles* which inspired

[1] *De Trinitate*, v. 10.

and controlled the formation of that Dogma. And in regard to these two factors it may be said that the *psychological motivations* may be worthy while the *philosophical or metaphysical principles* may be inadequate. As far as the first is concerned, the worthy concern of the Church was to guard and conserve the *eternal implications* of the historic facts : as far as the second is concerned, the acceptance of the finality and absoluteness of a " substance " metaphysic, it may be suggested, led her to a false emphasis—an emphasis which led her further and further away from the historic facts themselves. The Church was devoted, and rightly devoted, to the task of proclaiming an eternal message of God to men ; but her simultaneous devotion to the categories of Greek metaphysics left the " eternity " of that message to the mercy of an all-sufficient rationalism. It might even be suggested, as it has by many recent students, that this rationalism was in essence " materialistic." The recognition of this " materialistic " basis for Christological Dogma by some of the Church's ecclesiastical leaders of to-day presents a situation of

distinct urgency.[1]   It is obviously impossible
to acquiesce in a mere " incoherence," or in

[1] This issue was discussed with real insight and acute-
ness by the late Dr. W. Morgan in an article " Back to
Christ " in *D.C.G.* The basal conception underlying
the formulas of Nicæa and Chalcedon was that of Substance. " God is conceived primarily as the Absolute
Substance ; that is to say, as the indeterminate, unchanging and permanent ground of the knowable world of
variety, change and transience. Christ is true God
because He shares in the Divine Substance ; and because He has taken up human nature or substance into
union with His Divine Substance, He is also true man.
The inner relations at the Godhead—Fatherhood,
Sonship, the Procession of the Holy Spirit—are all
expressed in terms of this category. . . . Now, what
is this idea of Substance which plays so great a rôle
in the creeds ?   It was not derived from Christ or the
New Testament. It was borrowed from hellenistic
philosophy ; and what it originally answered was not
any religious need, but the purely intellectual demand
that all the manifoldness of this time-world shall be
reducible to the unity of a single principle. . . . Absolute Substance has nothing in common with the holy,
personal Will of the prophets, or with the gracious
Father of our Lord Jesus Christ. . . . To substitute
a divinity of Substance for a divinity of Revelation is
to remove Christ from the realm of faith into that of
speculation ; and, further, *since the category of substance
is at bottom a physical category*, it is to rank the physical
above the personal and ethical." Space forbids my

a " materialistic " foundation for a doctrinal statement. The Church is, surely, called to the task of re-thinking the theological implications of the Gospel. Perhaps the supreme peril here is fear. In a world of change fear may so easily issue in a state of nerveless inaction. There is a danger to-day

instancing many less weighty, and more recent, recognitions of this " materialistic " basis.

As far as the Chalcedonian statement on the Person of Christ is concerned, its " incoherent " nature is widely and frankly recognised to-day. Among the many statements I might cite, I take the following from Dr. H. R. Mackintosh : " The Council (i.e. Chalcedon) did not so much reconcile or synthesise the opposing theories put before it, as conceal their opposition under extremely careful phrases " (*The Person of Jesus Christ*, p. 215). Dr. W. P. Paterson, also, recognises that the Chalcedonian definition is " beset by very grave intellectual difficulties," and that its " self-consistency " is " open to question" (*The Rule of Faith*, pp. 227-8).

The best that can be said for this formula is that in a difficult practical situation it enabled the Church to shelter heterogeneous Christologies. This claim cannot to-day be made for the formula, however divergent the present Christologies of the Church. For to-day, it is not just the question of a statement which is not coherent : it is that the statement has a quasi-physical foundation. In such an " abstract " foundation—devoid of real values—no Christian can acquiesce.

that lip-service should be given to the " in-adequacy " of doctrinal formulas without any corresponding endeavour to achieve less inadequate formulas. The acid test of the *sincerity* of our statements about dogmatic inadequacies is our endeavour to remove these. The issues involved are many and difficult : and there is a natural caution, which commands general and deep sympathy, lest the baby should be emptied out with the bath water—to use the familiar metaphor. Nevertheless, this caution does not absolve us from the duty of throwing away water that has lost its freshness or its purity, and is no longer healthy to the baby. The chief factor that has contaminated the water is, I believe, the rationalistic notion that a metaphysical formula is adequate to re-ligion itself. The speculative mind became so anxious to explain Jesus that it lost Jesus. He disappeared behind the famous Chalcedon-ian Definition, where " One and the same Christ " is " acknowledged in Two Natures unconfusedly (ἀσυγχύτως), unchangeably (ἀτρέπτως), indivisibly (ἀδιαιρέτως), insepar-ably (ἀχωρίστως)." Such a definition begins with a metaphysic of the disparateness of Divine and human "natures," and then seeks to accommodate the Jesus of history and the Gospel he incarnated to it, instead of beginning with the facts of history and experience and deciding the formula accordingly. As Dr. Garvie has very well said: " The inconsistencies of the creed show that abstract philosophical formulæ cannot do justice to historical reality." [1] This, however, was not the whole trouble caused by these statements. Not only is the Jesus of history obscured, but a conception of religion itself arises which is at fundamental variance with the religion he lived and taught. It comes to be thought that to be a Christian the first necessity is to give intellectual assent to doctrinal affirmations. The contribution

[1] *The Christian Doctrine of God*, p. 134. It is interesting and significant to note that this " disparateness " was accepted by the compilers of the Unitarian Racovian Catechism. Their reason for not accepting the doctrine that in Christ there was " the very essence of God " was thus expressed : " Two substances endued with opposite and discordant properties, such as are God and man, cannot be ascribed to one and the same individual, much less be predicated the one of the other."

of the Greek genius to Christianity, it must be admitted, was not unmixed gain. The endeavour to sum up the whole truth about God and Jesus in systematic statement and metaphysical formula led away from an experiential to a speculative emphasis : so that the test of one's Christianity became the holding of orthodox opinions, instead of a life of faith and of obedience.

Happily, however, the recognition of the inadequacy and unworthiness of the traditional Christological formulations has come at a time when the Church has been brought back to the historic facts of the life of Jesus. In such a synchronisation may we not see an over-ruling Divine Guidance ? For if, as I cannot but believe, the Church is being called to re-think the issues which were supposed to be finally decided in the fourth and fifth centuries, what more necessary than that she should begin with the Jesus of history ? He is the real starting-point of the Christian movement. And, beginning from that starting-point, we shall need to retrace the road which the Church took, noting the wrong turnings taken which led to the formation of dogma in terms "essentially materialistic." In approaching this re-reading and re-thinking, our outstanding gain is that through the labours of the Church's critical students we have been able to penetrate behind a philosophical abstraction to a living man.

But now—and herein is the striking resemblance of our situation to that which the Johannine author confronted—the recovery of the historic Jesus by critical research, while indispensable for the Church's task of thought, raises its own peculiar perplexities. These perplexities all come down to one main perplexity—*how to conceive of the historical in relation to the eternal, and the eternal in relation to the historical :* Or, to put the issue in other words, how to discover, and state, a Gospel *of God*—and a Gospel that is not God's Gospel is no Gospel at all—in and through the life and teaching of a man. Or, to put the issue in yet other words, how to maintain that there is anything Final in Christianity when it had its origin in the phenomenal.

This perplexity is one that belongs not only to Christianity but to every great philosophic system and to such great ethnic religions as those of Hinduism and Buddhism. How to see Eternal Meaning in the phenomenal and transitory, is the question of all the ages. As far as Christianity is concerned there are, I believe, three main ways of answering this question, and these three same ways can be seen in the Eastern religions as well. The first way is by denying the historical : this is the Gnostic way. The second way is by placing the eternal as a kind of static addendum to the historical : this is the way of " materialistic " orthodoxy and of the old " evidences " apologetic. The third way is by finding the eternal *in* the historical : this is the Johannine way.

In these and the coming days each of these ways will be tried, as they have in the past been tried. It would almost seem that each method of approach, through the congenital diversity of minds, persists through successive ages, in the environment also of some non-Christian religions. Most of the " isms " with which we are familiar in Christianity are found in the indigenous garb of the several ethnic religions, whether fundamentalism— or authoritarianism — modernism, ethicism,

rationalism, mysticism. As far as Christianity
is concerned, which is our interest here, the
perplexity arising from the difficulty of finding
the supernatural in the natural, the eternal
in the transitory, may be expected to lead
some to present a Christianity sundered from
the historical. Many are tempted, if I may
use the words of Professor Kittel, to surrender " the investigation of the past to the
experience of the present. Having drunk
the last drop from the cup of history and
found that it left only a nasty taste of re-
lativity, they will have no more of this
beverage and will seek purer draughts from
the timeless truths of æsthetics and liturgical
worship, in myths and symbols, where they
are disturbed by no history." [1] Such historical despair may represent not simply the
Gnostic attitude—which, indeed, is better
represented by the phrase " historical unconcern "—but the attitude of sincere, though
blind, critical investigators.

My suggestion is that the person of Jesus
will always elude critical research, unless that
research is accompanied with a Johannine

[1] In *Mysterium Christi* (ed. by Bell), p. 45.

insight into the unique religious consciousness
of Jesus. We have never really recovered
the historical Jesus until we have perceived,
however dimly, his secret. Historical research requires the highest faculties of spiritual
insight if it is to reach its goal. " Tan-
tum Jesus cognoscitur, quantum diligitur " :
" Jesus is known in proportion as he is loved."
The old Latin word contains, I believe, a true
canon for historical investigation of the person of Jesus. The deeper depths within *him*
call to the depths within ourselves. And
unless we ourselves have come to know
something of the spiritual and eternal within
ourselves, however weak and hesitating and
fleeting the perception is, we cannot hope to
discover it in the intimate and dominating
and constant assurance that it had for him.
His words about his knowledge of the Father
will come with vital and assuring meaning
to those to whom they represent a reality
known, however dimly, to themselves. " My
sheep," he said, " hear my voice " (see Jn. x.
3, 4, 14, 16). This is a hard saying. But
it is one of those hard sayings whose truth
is ultimately inescapable.

The Johannine emphasis and method of approach, therefore, has an abiding message both to those who have a Gnostic unconcern for history and to those who are afflicted by the historical despair of some critical investigators. It is only as we have penetrated to the filial consciousness of Jesus that, on the one hand, we really know the historic Jesus, and that, on the other hand, we can escape from the evanescent into the eternal, from the natural into the supernatural, from the material into the spiritual.

It is, I think, obvious that if either of the above positions were to prevail essential Christianity, as we have known it through the centuries from primitive Apostolic times, would have disappeared. Should it ever come to be universally believed that we must resign ourselves to agnosticism as to the mind of Jesus, or that the historical does not reveal the essentially Divine and Eternal, the main link will have been broken which has up to the present bound together the whole Christian movement. The link, indeed, has been broken in two places. With the first break—the break which follows an agnostic

conclusion as to the inmost mind of Jesus—
would go the specific message of Christianity ;
with the second break—the break involved
by Gnosticism—would go the essential message
of religion itself.

Let me seek to expound these two conten-
tions with greater precision.

Firstly, there is the issue raised by historical
agnosticism, or, as it might be termed, historical despair. Now, the specific message
of Christianity all through the centuries has
been the message of the Historic Incarnation.
This message has been expressed in many
different ways, and by the use of many figures
of speech. It is not always recognised that
every endeavour to set forth this belief in
human language is necessarily symbolical or
metaphorical ; but so it is. Before the Johannine author had written his Gospel Paul had
sought to express the truth in his words to the
Corinthian Christians : " God was in Christ
reconciling the world into Himself " (2 Cor.
v. 19). Here Paul made use of a *spatial*
figure to convey his belief. The Johannine
author's way of expressing the message was
no less metaphorical, different though the

metaphor was. " The Word became flesh and dwelt among us," he wrote. This is a figure of *genetic identification*, as I might venture to call it. The words, at least as translated in our versions, suggest that " the Word " came by some generative process to be identical with " flesh." Obviously the writer did not mean his words to be understood in so literal and unimaginative way. It would take us nearer to his meaning to translate " The word became *as* flesh." The term " incarnation " is itself figurative, in so far as it contains, like the Pauline utterance quoted above, the *spatial* preposition " in." Such symbolical language is, therefore, unavoidable ; and the remembrance of this fact will deliver us from following in the footsteps of many shortsighted polemical writers who have fought for, and about, figurative language, mistaking it for the reality it clothed. Nevertheless, the symbolical phrase, " the Historic Incarnation," *does symbolise something*, impossible though we may find the task of expressing it in non-figurative language. And whatever verbal expression we give to the belief, it means this at least, that we recognise

9

in the historic Jesus a unique manifestation of the Divine and the Eternal. Now, such a statement presupposes that we know what we mean when we say " the historic Jesus." If we do not know who Jesus was, especially if we do not know his inmost mind, the phrase " the historic Jesus " means nothing to us. We have, therefore, on the hypothesis of historical agnosticism, precluded ourselves from the very possibility of making the central Christian affirmation of " the Historic Incarnation." In an intimate theological discussion which took place some time ago, when what the present writer would regard as the fantastic " Christ-Myth " theory was under consideration, a critical historian of the Form-History school who was present said : " The theory *may* be true." It is in no wise in order to betray the intimacies of candid discussion,—as I hope will be understood—that such an incident is mentioned : no doubt such remarks are frequently made. What it is necessary should be maintained is that such avowals of historical agnosticism as to the person of Jesus involve the impossibility of maintaining the

Church's doctrine of "the Historic Incarnation." And if, as has been here suggested, the Church's thinkers are being called to rethink Christological Dogma the point of departure must be a Jesus who is known. And if in that historic Jesus there is no unique experience of God then it is impossible to reach from that starting-point *any* kind of Christological statement. Whatever Christological statement the future may reach, it can have no valid basis unless we have assurance that *in the experience of Jesus himself* God is uniquely known. It will not suffice, for such a basis, to declare that *we* have found a unique experience of God as mediated to us by Jesus. It cannot even suffice, for such a basis, to declare that we have communion with "the living Christ." Such declarations will have some valid place in such a basis. But, without the conviction that *in the consciousness of Jesus himself, in the whole experience which was his,* God was uniquely manifest, no kind of Christology is really possible. Any statement which wishes to retain the Christian message of "the Historic Incarnation" must rest upon known historic fact about the knowledge of God possessed by Jesus.

Secondly, there is the issue raised by modern forms of Gnosticism. In our own generation there has been a significant—though in point of volume and influence an insignificant—movement, in some ways having affinities with the Gnostic movement of the end of the first and the beginning of the second century,[1] I refer to the views of such writers as W. B. Smith and P. L. Couchoud. The underlying positions of the various "Christ-Myth" theorists differ considerably—sometimes fundamentally—and it is almost as difficult to decide their standing-ground as it is to decide that of the varied schools of early Gnostics.

In regard to these latter there is no modern agreement as to their precise position, and in some measure this lack of agreement is due to the fact that the Gnostic leaders of the second century are chiefly known through the "orthodox" writings of those who "refuted" them. One point, however, seems to be clear, namely, that those early Gnostics

[1] Two of the best recent accounts in English of the Gnostic movement are F. C. Burkitt's *Church and Gnosis* (1932), and A. C. McGiffert's *A History of Christian Thought* (1932), vol. i., bk. 1.

regarded themselves as Christians, even though it also seems clear that the main conceptions of Gnosticism did not *originate* in Christianity. In the words of Professor Burkitt, " the contest between Catholics and Gnostics was a struggle between persons who felt themselves to be Christians, not between Christians and heathens." [1] Wherein essentially did their position run counter to the position of the Church ? As far as I am able to understand their position, it lies here ; they could not believe that the Divine could be really manifest in a human Jesus. The physical was essentially evil. Jesus, who belonged to our world of sense and space and time, could not, therefore, reveal God. They endeavoured to secure the " Christianity " of their position by the theory that the Divine Aeon Christ came down and entered into Jesus the man. This theory, which at first sight has an " orthodox " ring about it, will be found upon reflection to make a Christian doctrine of Incarnation impossible. It is the heavenly being, to them, who manifests God, not the human Jesus. They could not

[1] *Church and Gnosis*, p. 8.

believe that the Divine and Eternal could be seen *in* and *through* the human and transitory. The Divine must be, as it were, *superimposed* upon the human ; the Eternal must be *added to* the transitory. The question of all the ages—whether here in time and space and sense, here in history, we can really " know " God and Eternity—is answered by the Gnostics in the negative. This is, I believe, the subtlest " heresy " the Church has ever been called to face ; and it is, I believe, the Johannine emphasis which alone delivers from its peril.

It is not here suggested that any of the modern " Christ-Myth " theorists adopt all the philosophical views of these early Gnostics. Some would *reject* them all. Rationalists such as the late Mr. J. M. Robertson have little or nothing in common with the esoteric mysticism of the second century Gnostics. Others, however, like Dr. Couchoud reveal some very deep-seated resemblances. The resemblances, it is important to note, are not on the precise question of historicity. They are on the question as to what we mean by the " spiritual," as to how the Divine

and Eternal is made known to us. There
is here a significant difference, and a significant agreement. The difference lies here.
Gnostics such as Marcion regarded the
humanity of Jesus as a mere appearance.
He was not born of a woman. His " death "
on the Cross was no real death. Nevertheless, the " humanity " of Jesus was *a historical
appearance ;* and the " death " of Jesus was
a historical appearance of death. This is
a significant difference in approach from that
of modern " Christ-Myth " theorists. For
the latter deny historicity even to what the
Gnostics regarded as " historical appearances."
The Gospel records, to the moderns, represent a later and retrograde " historicising "
of an earlier, and indeed primary, cult of a
heavenly Christ. The curious point about
this situation is that the Gnostics of the
second century are witnesses for the historicity
of the " appearances " they found in the
Gospels, and, therefore, furnish one of the
strongest arguments against modern " Christ-
Myth " theorists. There is also, however, a
significant agreement. It lies here ; in an
inability to believe that the Divine can be

manifest in the human, the Eternal in the
temporal. The agreement between, for example, Marcion and M. Couchoud is not the
agreement the latter claims. Marcion, he
tells us, found in St. Luke's Gospel " a spiritual
Jesus, not a Jesus of flesh and bone." And
he adds, " Let us read the Gospels as Marcion
read them." [1] Couchoud, as I have indicated,

[1] *Le Mystère de Jésus*, p. 183. For the best recent
discussion, from the standpoint of critical history, of
the modern Christ-Myth theory and its relationship to
Docetism, the reader may be referred to Prof. Maurice
Goguel's *Jésus de Nazareth : Mythe ou Histoire* (1925).
At the close of an acute discussion Goguel says :
" The Docetists did not contest the evangelical history.
They were Christian idealists, who, attached before
all else to the notion of the divinity of Christ and
of the heavenly nature of his person, sought to give
an interpretation of it which agreed with their ideas.
So understood, Docetism could only develop on the
terrain of the Gospel tradition. If the Docetists had
had the smallest reason to think that Christ was
but an ideal person without historical reality, they would
not have expended such treasures of ingenuity in order
to give an interpretation of his history which cut him
off completely from too immediate a contact with
humanity. The Docetists appear therefore as witnesses
of the Gospel tradition." (French edition, pp. 95-96.)
See also Goguel's recently published *Vie de Jésus*,
which includes the substance of the aforementioned
volume.

does not read the Gospels as Marcion read them : Marcion's reading explodes the modern Christ-Myth theory. Where Marcion and Couchoud are in agreement is in their conception of the Divine and the Spiritual. They both want " to leave the man and keep the god." [1] But the man Jesus cannot be left, nor can the " god " be found. The " spiritual reality " which Couchoud exhorts Christians to retain by the surrender of the human and historical reality is the myth of a non-existent Christ.[2]

To such views, bizarre though they be, it is worth while referring, inasmuch as such a reference reminds us of the historical situation to which the Johannine author

[1] *Le Mystère de Jésus*, p. 185.

[2] Couchoud concludes his volume with a seemingly ardent appeal to Christian historians, which reveals a Gnostic fervour allied to a historical obtuseness : " You can no longer materialise Jesus without obliterating him, and destroying him. . . . Will you be afraid of a spiritual reality, you whose noble function it is to maintain the reality of the spiritual ? Trust not to a doubtful legend. What you take for the haven is a mortal gulf. Haul up the sails ! Make for the deep, where to you it seems the tempest blows ! Those waves will bear you, men of little faith " (p. 186).

wrote with so abidingly valuable a message. When he wrote, " The Word became flesh," all Gnostic views were definitely excluded. Marcion recognised this quite clearly, for when he drew up his canon of the New Testament he excluded our Fourth Gospel, significantly including only ten epistles of Paul, and Luke's Gospel, which he regarded as Pauline. (We are reminded of Harnack's famous saying that Marcion was the only second-century writer who took the trouble to understand Paul and that he misunderstood him.[1]) Clement, in a well-known and much-quoted passage, preserved to us by Eusebius[2] from the lost *Hypotyposes*, tells us that " John, last of all, perceiving that what had reference to the body in the gospel of our Saviour was sufficiently detailed, and being encouraged by his familiar friends, and urged by the Spirit, wrote *a spiritual gospel*." Such a conception of " a spiritual Gospel " is poles apart from a Gnostic con-

[1] See article by Harnack on "Marcion" in *Encyclopædia Britannica*, eleventh edition ; also his *History of Dogma*, vol. i.

[2] *H.E.*, vi. 14.

ception of " a spiritual Gospel." The Johannine answer to the Gnostic conception of
a " spiritual " Gospel is that the " spiritual "
was manifest in the historic Jesus, and this
perception of the " spiritual " in Jesus was
known to the author by his own spiritual
perception. The Gospel is "spiritual," primarily in the historic spiritual reality to which
it witnessed, and secondarily in the spiritual
insight of the author which penetrated to
this secret. And so when a modern Gnostic
like Couchoud declares, after quoting the
beautiful passage from John x. 14-18, where
Jesus is portrayed as saying " I am the good
shepherd," etc., that " he who speaks thus
is the god of the Mystery," [1] the truly
" spiritual" interpretation of the passage is
that there speaks here the consciousness and
claim of the historic Jesus. And the " knowledge " of the eternal possessed by the Johannine author is not an esoteric knowledge of
a cult-Christ, but a " knowledge " of spiritual
reality manifest in a Jesus of history. " This,"
he said, " is life eternal that we might know
thee, the only true God, and Jesus Christ

[1] *Op. cit.*, p. 173.

whom thou hast sent" (Jn. xvii. 3). It is a "spiritual" knowledge, not because it is divorced from a knowledge of the earthly, but because it penetrates to the secret of the earthly.

What, then, is the place for the Church's theological and Christological endeavours? Is it that this whole intellectual task of the Church is just one long-continued mistake? That is very far from the suggestions we have here made. The recognition of the *inadequacy* of a Chalcedonian Christological formulation does not mean that the endeavour after coherent statement was *in itself* wrong. The human mind being what it is, the task was inevitable. The history of theology is just the history of the mental life of the Church. The Gnostics themselves were among the first speculative theologians of the Christian movement. They were urged on by the essentially philosophic endeavour to think all things together. They thought *as Christians*, too, let us not forget—that is, as those who regarded themselves as Christians. They endeavoured to relate what they conceived as Christian history to cosmological theories which had come down to them. Those theories were dominated by their conception of evil, which they regarded as inherent in matter. And it was because they were so concerned to separate the Divine from what they regarded as this very evil world of time and space and sense, that they explained away the things of time and space and sense in the Gospel narrative of Jesus. Where the Gnostics went wrong, in the eyes of the Church, was in denying the obvious signi-ficance of the historic facts. This obvious significance *had* to be surrendered by them because it did not fit in with their cosmological speculative theories. These theories were de-terminative of the history, instead of the history being determinative of the theories.

Now, this brief sketch of the Gnostic Christological aberration should reveal clearly what must be the method of approach to all theological and Christological endeavour. It must be an approach *from* the historical *to* the speculative interpretation, not from the speculative interpretation to the historical. In other words, it must be inductive. The Church herself, as we have maintained, got further and further away from the historic facts when in the fourth and fifth centuries she made a "substance" metaphysic determinative of the Gospel of the Divine Word in Jesus. She who had repudiated Gnosticism in the second century because of its lack of fidelity to the historic facts, herself became guilty of a similar error. And so the Jesus of history was clouded behind a Christ of speculative dogma. The Church, if I may put the matter in other words, historicised her metaphysical concepts and regarded the result as the historic Jesus. The lesson from all this is surely this : that our future Christologies must be based on the historic fact of Jesus, and must never obscure him. If they obscure him they are self-condemned.

It is when our Christologies become more concerned with a speculative metaphysical unification than with the fact of the whole religious experience of Jesus and of the Church that they go wrong. It is not that the quest for unification is itself wrong : it is that it is directed by the wrong leader. The only guide to a Christian unification is the authoritative guide of the whole religious consciousness of Jesus. If the "leader" in the quest becomes a rationalistic meta-physic we shall have reached a goal far removed from our real goal, and in the journey shall have lost sight of our real guide. Our Christological theories must arise out of our rational reflections upon the whole mind and consciousness of Jesus. The only adequate source for a Christian doctrine of the Incarnation is the self-proclamation of his inner consciousness.

But, says the rationalist within us, is not this to leave the Incarnation "undemon-strated"? *It is*, in the *rationalist* sense— but not, I would suggest, in the *rational* sense. The difference between the two ad-jectives is that the former claims a complete self-sufficiency, while the latter recognises its place within the inseparable unity of the whole deep, many-sided personal life. The former would *control* the experiences which life gives to us; the latter perceives that it is *controlled* by life and its environment. And so the "rationalist" can never "prove" the Incarnation, as he cannot "prove" any of the fundamental presuppositions which give meaning to life. Any Christological statement which is based on the supposition that it should be so presented as to be capable of " proof " is founded upon a self-sufficient rationalism. The Incarnation by its very nature is incapable of rationalistic demonstration. For here the assertion is made that *God* is uniquely manifest in the man Jesus. If God Himself is incapable of rationalistic demonstration, so also is this assertion. Nevertheless, the doctrine of the Incarnation can be so stated as to be seen to be truly *rational*. Its rationality receives the only " demonstration " of which any such doctrine is susceptible, when it is so presented as to give coherence and meaning to all the facts of life. *Credo ut intelligam*—which might be freely paraphrased : *my belief makes life and the universe intelligible*. This is what Browning meant when he said in his well-known words from *A Death in the Desert* :

I say the acknowledgment of God in Christ
Accepted by thy reason, solves for thee
All questions in the earth and out of it.

I do not suppose that Browning meant, when he said this, that " all questions " received, thus, an answer completely satisfactory to a self-sufficient rationalism. The whole context of his thought shows that such an interpretation was very far removed from his position. What he says is that the questions involved in the whole temporal and eternal, earthly and heavenly, experiences of life itself are found to have a rational answer within the context of the incarnational belief. The Incarnation is " rational," in the same sense as Theism is " rational." It is the belief in God which gives adequate meaning to the facts of life and of the universe : but this does not mean that the belief in God gives an answer that will be regarded as satisfying to all the questions raised by an impoverishing rationalism. Life is bigger and richer than thought : and thought has to explain, not explain away, the richness and sublimity of life. It is in this same sense that the acknowledgment of God in Christ explains, without explaining away, the experiences of life itself.

My suggestion has been that the doctrine

of the Incarnation can only be so presented when deep within the whole religious consciousness of Jesus God is perceived. This is a "rational" but not a "rationalistic" method of approach. It is an approach which does not deride reason ; to do that would be to take a long step to scepticism. But it is an approach which refuses to make the human intellect the measure of all things ; to do this last would be to take an even longer step to the same sceptical goal.

The main test of any Christological statement is whether it clarifies and illumines or distorts and obscures the Divine as revealed in Jesus. If it clouds that revelation it is self-condemned. If it illumines it and shows its "reasonableness" it will fulfil a real and necessary function. That function is to mark the centrality of the Jesus of history in the whole Christian movement. It must not itself usurp the central place : such a usurpation leads to all kinds of positions which are incompatible with his spirit and teaching— to the "Anathemas" of an Athanasian Creed, and to the persecuting zeal which has characterised many branches of the Church bearing his name. It will little avail the Christianity of the future to achieve a new Christological formula if it does not spring from a direct vision of the mind of Jesus and a penetrating insight into his eternal meaning and value. Our formulas have only worth in so far as they translate his life and experience into the language of coherent thought.

If we resign " incoherent " statements, that does not mean that we resign the vital belief which is at their heart. On the other hand, to refuse to relinquish mere " incoherences " is a counsel of despair, and involves the ultimate relinquishment, not merely of untenable formulas, but of the central belief within the formulas. History, happily, tells us how the ultimate beliefs of humanity have survived many of the untenable arguments by which they were supported and expressed. And the real reason why the Christian belief in the " Historic Incarnation " has outlived many of the inadequate arguments and formulas by which it has been buttressed is that its vitalising centre has been a Johannine insight into the unique manifestation of the Eternal and Divine in the person of Jesus.

(II) *The Message of essential Mysticism.*— It is obvious that if our interpretation of the Fourth Gospel is the right interpretation the author was in the truest and best sense a " mystic." It is further obvious that in here maintaining that this Gospel has an *abiding message* we are presupposing that such a " mysticism " belongs to the very core of Christianity. It is therefore desirable that this issue should be considered with greater precision, and, especially, with reference to some of the varied modern objections which are brought against the mystical approach to religion, and the mystical element in it.

It is, I think, significant that the Christian mystics of all the centuries have found themselves " at home " in this Gospel. From Clement of Alexandria to the Cambridge Platonists, from Origen to the Quakers, from Irenaeus to Fénélon, the language and figures of this book have been a staple of their thought. In all " mystical " writings we are continually meeting with such Johannine words as Light, Love, Word, Way, Life, to describe the Divine and Its penetration of the human spirit, and such verbs as "to abide," "to dwell," "to be one with," to express the nature of this experience. In our own day every thoughtful mind must have noticed that all those Christians whom we regard as, in a vague and general way, "mystical" have a natural affinity for this Gospel. Such a consensus of witness, both reasoned and, which is perhaps even more significant, unreasoned, points to the "justness" of a "mystical" interpretation of the Gospel.

But what precisely is this "mysticism"? There are few words in the vocabulary of religion that arouse stronger approvals and antipathies than this word. It might be well if the word could be forgotten for a few generations, and attention concentrated upon what the "mystics" were really trying to say. Dean Inge in his Bampton Lectures gives a series of twenty-six definitions ; the number of the definitions is suggestive, being equal to the number of letters in our alphabet. Mysticism is variously regarded as belonging to the earliest and lowest stages of mental development, or to the last and highest. There

are theologians who cannot regard it as other
than a pathological state. To some it is the
"last enemy" of Christianity, and in this
they have found themselves at one with
rationalist materialists.[1] And in every age
there are found Christian thinkers who regard
it as of the essence of their religion.

I will not here immerse myself in a discussion about *words ;* I have no interest in
using such a word as "mysticism" either as
a ninepin which I can, to my own satisfaction,
knock down, or as a shield with which I can
ward off inquirers from the sanctity of my
own personal faith.

What I wish to say is that religion claims
a direct knowledge of God. Involved in it
is what Rufus Jones calls "an immediate
awareness of relation with God, a direct and
immediate consciousness of the divine presence."[2] It is not just a discursive knowledge *about* God. If it were, the word might,

---

[1] Cf. the view of the late Dr. B. B. Warfield. In
his posthumous *Studies of Theology,*—in the last paper
on Mysticism—he says : "We may be mystics or we
may be Christians. We cannot be both."

[2] *Studies in Mystical Religion*, p. xv.

to the convenient clarification of issues, very well disappear : for such a word as " theology," or such a phrase as " philosophy of religion," would cover all that requires to be said. And in that case the measure of our religion would be the measure of our theological or philosophical understanding. We should thus be compelled to acquiesce in such a statement as the following which I take from Fichte's *Lectures on the Way Towards the Blessed Life*, delivered at Berlin in 1806 : "Only through a systematic study of philosophy is it possible for man to elevate himself to Religion and its blessings, and every one who is not a philosopher must remain for ever shut out from God and his kingdom."[1] This is another hard saying, and if its truth were substantiated by the facts and experiences of life, we should be compelled to acquiesce in it, and, indeed, approve it warmly—which is, after all, the acid test of acquiescing in truth. All our experience of life, however, shows that "religion" is not the monopoly of theologians or philosophers ; few would even suggest that its most conspicuous manifestation has

[1] See Fichte's Popular Works, E.T., vol. ii., p. 315.

been there seen. "The wise and understanding" have been frequently strangers
to the truths of the Kingdom, truths known
to "the babes." With full approval we can
agree with some later words of Fichte, whom
I am glad to quote again : "Herein Religion
does consist, that man in his own person
and not through that of another, should
immediately behold, have, and possess God."
"This, however, is possible," he adds, "only
by means of pure, independent Thought, for
only through this does man assume true and
real personality, and this alone is the eye to
which God can become visible." [1]   This latter
statement is only true if in " pure, independent
Thought " is included, not only the " thought "
of the discursive intellect, but the " thought "
of intuitive and direct apprehension.

Theology is no more religion than geology
is the earth or psychology is the mind. Philosophy itself is based upon subject-matter
given in experience, and the endeavour to
lift itself into a region above the " subjectivities " of human experience is as futile
as trying to pull oneself into the air by one's

[1] *Op. cit.*, p. 316.

boot laces, or like expecting to keep above *terra firma* when sawing through the branch of the tree on which one is sitting. These "subjectivities" of human experience *are* the stuff of which religion is made, whether we like it or not. We can only talk about religion because there have been men and women who have been religious. To discuss it as if it were an abstraction about which one could argue without reference to the thoughts and experiences of real men, is akin to discussions on the anatomy of a centaur. All theology, and all philosophy of religion, presuppose religious experiences which have belonged to real men. And what I am here concerned to maintain is that the *body* of this experience has been the claim to communion with the Divine, to knowledge of the Eternal. If this claim had never been made we should not have had the word "religion" coming down to us, with its distinctness of meaning from such terms as theology and philosophy.

What we call Science and Theology and Philosophy are the result of intellectual operations. They differ in the realm of experience

with which they deal, and this difference
of realm determines the different methods
by which they deal with their subject-matter.
But what should never be forgotten is that
in each the subject-matter is human experience, and in each it is the human mind that
deals with this experience. The endeavour
to lift any one of these into a sacrosanct
realm where it cannot be subjected to the
scrutiny and reflection of the mind which
has had this experience is of all tasks the most
futile.   It is just the endeavour to ward off
the mind from itself, with the warding off
done by the mind itself.   In such a process
we merely see the human mind disguising
itself in three different garbs—like the actor
who appears on the stage, now as the hero,
now as the villain, now as the judge.   But
when it comes to the final scene, when the
judge is supposed to try the villain for attempt-
ing the life of the hero—the attempt having
been made off the stage—it is discovered
that the trial cannot be staged, for the three
are one.

When this is remembered, it will be seen
that all discursive thought presupposes ex-

periences about which it thinks. The mind can only think when there is something to think about, when, in other words, there is *subject* and *object*. The object, however, is never merely object, for it can only be known by a subject. What the mind thinks about, therefore, is some part of its environment which has become known to itself in consciousness. So it is with theology and the philosophy of religion. They are concerned with the co-ordination and interpretation of man's religious experiences. For either to deny that these experiences have any validity in and by themselves is like a man putting his own head voluntarily under the guillotine.

The personal, direct vision of God is the vital nerve of all religion. Should that be lost no hypothesis, however seemingly cogent, will secure religion's continued existence in the world. Such a situation would be like trying to comfort a man who has lost the affection of his wife by demonstrating to him that it *once* existed. The future of religion in the world is the future of direct apprehension of God, intuitive vision of God.

Theology, which might be defined as philosophy inspired and controlled by religious experience, has its necessary function—as has been already here maintained. But here again it must not be forgotten that there is only theology when there are theologians. Now a theologian can only consider his subject-matter with any competence or understanding if he himself has personal experience of what religious people have been saying. Failing this, he will seek to explain, either as Dogma or as fiction, what they have been saying. But what he will never be able to capture is the essential nature of the experiences themselves.

As I am seeking here to relate the Johannine message and emphasis to significant features of the modern situation, I may be permitted to refer to one of the strongest, and certainly most logically compact, recent statements of the theistic position. Dr. Tennant, in his closely reasoned study of *Philosophical Theology*,[1] is profoundly unsympathetic and

[1] *Philosophical Theology* (vol. i., 1928 ; vol. ii., 1930) ; see also the same author's *Miracle and its Philosophical Presuppositions* (1925), where an *a priori* defence of

exceedingly critical of this whole claim made
by men through all the ages to have a direct
vision of God. His position, precisely stated,
is to call in question the validity of this claim.
The way of immediate religious experience
is a " no thoroughfare " to theism.[1] Mystic
experiences " vouch nothing beyond their
own occurrence "[2]—to which the materialist
and the pantheist may be expected to reply
in similar vein to the theist's evidences. He
holds that such validity can be established
only as " reasonable inference from discursive
' knowledge ' about the world, human history,
the soul with its faculties and capacities ;
and above all, from knowledge of the inter-
connections between such items of knowledge." [3]

The crux of the question is the question
as to what is meant by " validity." If
there is only " validity " when discursive

the absolute *miraculum* is supported by the denial of
the validity of the *religious* sense of the supernatural ;
and also *Philosophy of the Sciences* (1932), where the
substance of the position of *Philosophical Theology* is
maintained, if in more guarded language.

[1] *Phil. Theol.*, vol. i., p. 311.
[2] *Op. cit.*, vol. i., p. 317.   [3] *Op. cit.*, vol. i., p. 325.

thought has satisfactorily dealt with all the
facts of human experience, we shall indeed
have a long time to wait before any " validity "
anywhere has been reached. Such a conception of " validity " is, I would suggest, a
rationalistic conception of validity. It seems
to me to be based upon the latent conviction
that man's discursive intellect is the measure
of the universe. And yet every one knows
that having reached our hypothesis of our
validly-believed-in God, we should have lost
Him for ever. " Le Dieu défini, c'est le Dieu
fini." Religion, however, as I understand it,
denies that the discursive intellect is the only
test of " validity." There is the validity of
direct vision, of—I will even venture the
adjective—*immediate* apprehension of God.
This word " immediate," which seems to
cause a good deal of misgiving to some, is
a word that religion will not drop from its
vocabulary in spite of all assaults made upon
it.   It does not mean that an experience
of God is claimed which has not been
" mediated " by the functions of our personal
being. No one, I trust, is so stupid as to
claim a knowledge of anything—whether it

be of a table, a sonata, a poem, a sunset—
without the mediation involved in the trans-
ference from object to subject. If we know
we can only know through our faculties.
But the whole question is whether there is
any activity of the spirit of man whereby
he can know, not *about* God, but *know* God.
And it is to such an experience that the religious man gives the term " *immediate* experience." The only person who can believe
in the " immediacy " of " unmediatedness "
is the complete Deist, to whom " inspiration "
is as the handwriting on the wall of the mind,
the *ab extra* intervention of the Divine upon
an utterly undivine world. And, in point
of the most obvious fact, those who have
least sympathy with any Deism are they
who believe that they have heard the very
voice of God, have seen the very vision of
Him.

Dr. Tennant uses an analogy to support
his contention. He says : " It should to-day
be as little necessary to ascertain, by first-
hand study, the nature of mystical experience, before calling its alleged philosophical
import in question, as to repeat for oneself

Galileo's experiments, before venturing to hazard statements as to falling bodies."[1] The analogy, however, is inappropriate to the subject under discussion. For the point is that while Galileo's experiments need not be repeated by anyone who affirms statements based upon the truth of those experiments, yet every one believes that he *can* verify those statements, if he will undertake the task. But those who have the sense of the presence of God do not claim that it can be verified at will. The conditions for a Galileo's experiment are constant factors—if I may venture to regard a leaning tower as a constant factor. The conditions of "mystic experience" are not objectively-constant factors ; they are "subjective" factors. And though the "mystic" claims no monopoly of his experience, he is ever stressing the subjective conditions that have to be observed before the experience can be found. The repetition of Galileo's experiments is on a totally different plane from a "first-hand study" of "mystic experience." The one belongs to the realm of phenomenal fact ;

[1] *Op. cit.*, vol. i., p. 315.

" mystic experience " belongs to the realm
of religious fact. Strictly speaking, there is
no such thing as " first-hand study " of religious experience. Such " first-hand study "
is always really second-hand. There is a
" first-hand " experience, and there is a
" second-hand " study of that experience.
And, failing a first-hand experience, no second-
hand study can penetrate to the real subject-
matter.

Nor does the claim that religious experience makes for itself mean, to use the profoundly unsympathetic words spoken by Victor
Cousin in reference to " mysticism," that it
is " the most implacable enemy of reason . . .
so that according as one or the other prevails,
religion is reasonable or absurd." [1] Whoever
frees us from a self-sufficient self-esteem is
not our " enemy " ; he is usually our best
friend, difficult though we may find it to believe this at the time. And the real friend
of " reason " is that religious experience
which, in transcending the human reason,

[1] See his discussion of *Religion, Mysticism, Stoicism*,
translated with other Philosophical Miscellanies from
the French in 2 vols. (Boston, 1838), vol. i., p. 169.

gives coherence and meaning to all the facts of life and of the universe.

It is out of the whole depth of human experience that logical reasoning springs. Beyond the reach of man's intellectual faculty there is a realm of experience which may be known to the mind in its wholeness. The function of the reason is to analyse the entirety of experience ; and in this necessary task it will show that some so-called mystics have made exorbitant claims for their experience. They have sometimes imagined that the details of their theological creed were validated by their direct religious vision— such a dogma, for example, as that of the Trinity has occasionally been held to be " given " in direct religious experience. Such exorbitant claims, it is well to remember, have not been confined to the so-called mystics. In the writings of all " rationalists " and all materialists, even more strikingly exorbitant claims have been made. But we do not, on that account, deny to the intellect of man a right and necessary function. So neither should we deny that direct religious experience has a validity of its own because of the extravagant credal claims made by some whose intellectual capacity was not highly developed. There is an *immediate* knowledge of God which comes otherwise than through the mediation of man's conscious ratiocinative processes. To allow such processes to be the sole arbiter of the validity of such knowledge is, in the last resort, more ruinous than the most extravagant excesses of the " mystics." Let the intellect seek to clarify, if it can, the intuitions of direct religious vision ; but let it not deny that there is anything to clarify. The supreme indebtedness of religious humanity through all the ages is to the prophets and the " mystics." Without them there would be no philosophical theology. No valuation of religion which loses sight of this inheritance is other than a devaluation. " If we cannot," we are reminded, " without begging the question at issue, positively repudiate the mystic's claim, and so must leave him invulnerable as to his private conviction, we can also leave him powerless to substantiate his claim." [1] This will seem to every religious seer very

[1] *Op. cit.*, vol. i., pp. 318-19.

much like a taunt. Our Lord, among others,
will have to be left " invulnerable in his private
conviction " of the reality of God known
directly in the depths of his personal consciousness. And that he was so left by
many is evident in the Johannine Gospel.

A theology that has no room for the direct
vision, the intuitive knowledge, the immediate
awareness, of God will never be other than
a truncation. It can never satisfy the heart
and mind of man.

> " *My busie, stirring heart that seekes the best,*
> *Can find no place on earth wherein to rest ;*
> *For God alone, the author of its bliss,*
> *Its onlie rest, its onlie centre is.*"

He who claims to " know " God is the very
first to declare that " His essence " is in-
comprehensible. The affirmation of a true
" religious agnosticism " has been most frequently made by those who have been usually
called the " mystics "—seldom by theologians
of the rationalist type. Here is a hymn
by Lange, translated by John Wesley—and
Wesley had some hard and unillumined things
to say about "mysticism " :

"O God, Thou bottomless Abyss!
Thee to perfection who can know?
O height immense! What words suffice
Thy countless attributes to show?"

Or consider a hymn by a religious poet of our own nation—Isaac Watts:

"God is a name my soul adores,
The almighty Three, the eternal One;
Nature and grace, with all their powers,
Confess the Infinite unknown."

Whether these writers are called "mystics" or not—and, again, the discussion is not about names—they acknowledge in their very claim to see Him and to know Him that His Being transcends all their faculties. All religious literature is full of this acknowledgment, not least the Bible of the Jews and the Bible of Christians. The name given to the Divine Being, which we magnificently mispronounce "Jehovah," had not to be uttered, and the Massoretic device for ensuring this—by vocalising יהוה, *JHVH*, with the vowels of אֲדֹנָי, *Adonai*, so that, in reading, the latter was substituted for the former—is familiar to students of the Old Testament. To Jacob's

question, "Tell me, I pray Thee, Thy name," no
answer, the narrator feels, can be given (Gen.
xxxii. 29). The nameless name of Jahveh given
to Moses is *I am that I am* or *I will be what
I will be* (Ex. iii. 14). This religious agnosticism expresses itself in the familiar words
of Zophar the Naamathite : " Canst thou
by searching find out God ? Canst thou
find out the Almighty unto perfection ? It is
high as heaven ; what canst thou do ? Deeper
than Sheol ; what canst thou know ? " (Job
xi. 7). The apocryphal book of Ecclesiasticus
gives expression to a similar recognition on
the part of its second century B.C. Palestinian
author : " We may say many things, yet
shall we not attain ; And the sum of our words
is, He is all. How shall we have strength
to glorify Him ? For He is Himself the great
one above all His works. The Lord is terrible
and exceeding great ; And marvellous is
His power. When ye glorify the Lord, exalt
Him as much as ye can ; For even yet will
He exceed : And when ye exalt Him, put forth
your full strength : Be not weary ; for ye
will never attain. Who hath seen Him, that
he may declare Him ? And who shall magnify

Him as He is ? Many things are hidden
greater than these ; For we have seen but
a few of His works. For the Lord made all
things ; And to the godly gave He wisdom "
(Ecclus. xliii. 27-33). In all first-hand religion there is the recognition of " ineffability."
This word itself is seldom if ever used save
in a religious context. Words are not adequate
to the richness and subtlety of experience.
When it is remembered that man's spiritual
nature has only been developing for a few
thousand years this fact will cease to cause
wonderment. The greater part of our human
language is concerned with what belongs
to physical and sensuous existence, as is
inevitable in the present low stage of
humanity's evolution. If spiritual development should continue at anything like the
rate shown during the last twenty or thirty
milleniums, in a few hundred thousand years
the balance of our language will be on the
side of the things unseen and intangible.
At present every religious mind struggles
almost desperately to express that which

" *lies far hidden from the reach of words.*"

It is filled with the sense of Worship and Adoration. He who is known within is always "Other." The language of religious experience, which ever claims to be "one" with God, is sometimes crudely interpreted as involving a claim to "identity" or "numerical oneness." A scrutiny of the innumerable passages in which those who have the "direct vision" bow before the Transcendent, would have saved rationalistic interpreters from this blunder. "Consistency" may be a virtue or a vice. It is a virtue when we refuse to allow logical contradictories in the realms for which logic is competent. It is a vice if it be thought that there is no realm beyond the determination of man's logical faculty. The clarity for which our minds so often seek is the clarity of the shallow stream. The important question in life is not, Have we seen clearly, but, *What* have we seen ?

*" He sees not clearliest, who sees all
    things clear."*

Poverty of mental content belongs more frequently to those who can put the truth of things into the nutshell of logical formulas,

than to those who recognise the " ineffable "
in the unplumbed depths of reality. Words
are not equal to the subtlety of things.

Because some of those who have been
called " mystics " have denied or mutilated
one function of their being, we are not called
to deny and mutilate *another*. Because some
have repudiated thinking, we shall not therefore repudiate our immediate sense of awareness, our intuitive apprehension of God.
Because some of those whose intellectual
faculties have been but slightly developed
have regarded their direct vision of God
as authenticating the details of their theological creed, we shall not therefore conclude
that such an experience authenticates nothing.
The religious insight we value is not that of
the Saracen in Scott's *Talisman :* " When our
reason in human things is disturbed or de-
stroyed, our view heavenward becomes more
acute and perfect." It is the insight, not of
the disordered reason, but of the reason which
recognises its own limitations. The continual
endeavour of the intellect is to submit to
dispassionate scrutiny the intimacies of the
religious experiences belonging to personal

consciousness, in order, if possible, to achieve general formulas to which every one may assent. But the formula is never the experience itself. To this the abstract thinker in every age finds it difficult to agree, and he is supported in his unwillingness by the desire for facile acquiescence in dogma by those who do not think at all. Adroitness in the manipulation of abstract notions is seldom indicative of true insight. Such cleverness reminds us of the juggler of our boyhood days. There is, however, this difference—the juggler in abstractions deceives not only his audience, but sometimes even himself.

It is obvious, further, that this direct religious insight has close affinities with that vivid apprehension which belongs to the true artist. He knows the possession of that moment when

> " *steady moods of thoughtfulness* " *are*
> " *matured*
> *To inspiration.*"

Often he travails for that moment. Not till it comes does he really see. It is when, having seen, he speaks—whether on canvas, in words, in music, in marble—that others

also are helped to see. It is vision that
quickens vision, spark that kindles spark.
For that reason, most " commentaries " on
the great works of genius puzzle rather than
inspire. Here and there we find the " com-
mentator " whose endeavour to " explain "
is controlled and inspired by the vision he
has himself received from his master. And
then his interpretation really illumines. But
in so many cases the endeavour to explain
leaves us wondering what there was to explain. A strenuous endeavour to make clear
to ourselves, or others, what we do not really
see is not inspiration. There is a certain
" unimpeded creativeness " which comes of
direct vision. It is then, as the late Mr.
C. E. Montagu so finely expressed it, that
" beauty comes without travail to the birth,
and the artist's own mind, or some part of it,
seems to look on at the happy miracle from
without, enchanted or awed by the strange,
uncalculated rightness of each effortless touch
that he gives to the thing that takes shape
in his hands." [1]

[1] See *C. E. Montagu : A Memoir*, by Oliver Elton
(1929), p. 298.

The greatest works of art have not come by hard, pedestrian intellectualisation. It is only when the intellect is inspired and controlled by direct insight that something is born which speaks to the world. Michael Angelo has first to *see* the curved poise of David in the block of apparently ruined marble before he can labour to the profit and joy of the generations. This is also true of the greatest scientific discoveries. They have been due to the flash of creative insight. It is then that all the puzzling data fall into place ; the "heap of stones" then becomes a house. These experiences of synthesising vision come like the Spirit in the Johannine Gospel : " The wind bloweth where it listeth, and thou hearest the sound thereof, but knoweth not whence it cometh, and whither it goeth : so is everyone that is born of the spirit " (iii. 8). The author, I have no doubt, knew of what he was writing : his Gospel is not the Q.E.D. of a chain of reasoning, it is the direct, creative vision which has fused the whole depth of his experience and given meaning and coherence to every idea reflected upon.

Those who tell us *what Life means* are not chiefly those who laboriously puzzle out its problems; they are those who truly *live*: not those who try, however desperately, to think its experiences together, but those who in personal life open up new chapters of experience: not those who put all truth into the nutshell of formulæ, but those who, following the Spirit of truth, press on to a goal that fades forever as they move. They do not systematise: they create. They do not " solve " the problem of existence: they make that problem luminous by the light that never was on land or sea. They are—to use a phrase suggested to me somewhere by von Hügel, but which for the moment I cannot trace to its source—the self-spending children of the dawn and of Christ's ampler day.

The claim of religion, then, is that there is such a thing as real communion with God. " Spirit to spirit Thou dost speak." It is not just belief in His existence. It is not just " the pressure of duty " upon the mind. God is not just a postulate, whether of the rational consciousness or of the moral consciousness. Religion speaks of an awareness of the whole spirit of the Father of spirits. The characteristic of every truly religious man is to know that God *is*, not that He *was :* to hear what He *says,* not to affirm what He *has said*. " Thus *saith* the Lord," is the voice of the prophet. God is the Living God : He acts here and now.

This claim involves what is usually called the " Immanence " of God. The word is used in many senses, as most of the words in this high realm are. Labelled " pantheism," it has been frequently set up as a convenient ninepin in order that it may cleverly be knocked down. The same might be said of the other term " Transcendence," in this case the label attached being " deism." Both the words, however, are completely inadequate to the reality they are used to express. Each word is involved in the notion of space, and space means nothing when applied to spirit. What the terms mean *to religion,* are experiences of the human spirit in its relation to God. They are not, *to religion,* theories of the universe. They are abstract terms, and religion is concerned with concrete experiences.

Since man must be theological as well as

religious, there is in every age a kind of ding-dong battle between Immanence and Transcendence. Theology is ever on its guard against Pantheism ; religion regards Deism as the great enemy. Belief in the aloof Artificer of Deism involves the death of all real religion ; and the death of real religion involves the death of all theology. So it would seem that the enemy of both religion and theology is Deism. If God is conceived as the external Creator of the universe, apart from which He dwells in remote, transcendent splendour, man could never *know* Him but only infer His existence from the universe He had made. Religion is then regarded as hanging precariously on these inferences. It is for this reason that a deistic conception of God always goes hand in hand with a rationalistic approach to religion. This " rationalism " has taken two forms in Christian history—the form which rests upon the finality and absoluteness of " dogmatic " statements, and the form which rests upon the logical validity of its own " proofs." But what is usually forgotten is that we should never have had any statements about God, and should never even *begin* to " prove " His existence, if He were just " wholly other." Even to say that God is transcendent involves that He is " Immanent."

It is significant that this emphasis on the " immanence " of God is found in the works of the world's greatest poets. Often their utterances have been interpreted by a hard rationalism as indicating that they were metaphysical " pantheists "; and no doubt much of the language of such poets as Goethe and Wordsworth is open to this misconception. Anyone who sees with piercing insight one aspect of truth *must* say it with an emphasis which lays him open to the charge that he has forgotten or denied other aspects. He seldom seeks the " nicely calculated more or less " of abstract discussion. Occasionally he himself becomes " dogmatic," as when he denies that there is any truth in the position of those who do not see what he sees, or of those who see something which he does not see. Shelley's famous pamphlet on *The Necessity of Atheism*, written as a young man at Cambridge, comes to my mind as an illustration of " dogmatic denial " on the

part of a true poet. The pamphlet concludes
with the words: "Every reflecting mind
must allow that there is no proof of the existence of a Deity, Q.E.D." The dogmatic
and contemptuous language which he used
in this early pamphlet can be understood as
an intense repudiation of the popular Deism
of his day. Goethe had expressed similar
convictions but in a positive form:

> "No! such a God my worship may not win
> Who lets the world about His finger spin
> A thing extern: my God must rule within,
> And whom I own for Father, God, Creator,
> Hold nature in Himself, Himself in nature;
> And in His kindly arms embraced, the
>   whole
> Doth live and move by His pervading soul."

In a hundred passages Wordsworth expresses
the same truth. God is "A Presence," and
not a mere inference, as he tells us in his lines
on Tintern Abbey. He knew the experience
of a "central peace subsisting at the heart of
endless agitation":

> "Our destiny, our being's heart and home,
> Is with infinitude, and only there."

12

The " transcendental feeling " which is conveyed by the world's greatest poetry springs from the immanental insight which belongs to religious experience.   It belonged to Emily Brontë when she sang in her last lines :

> " *O God within my breast,*
> *Almighty, ever-present Deity !*
> *Life—that in me has rest,*
> *As I—undying Life—have power in*
> *Thee !*
>
> " *Though earth and man were gone,*
> *And suns and universes ceased to be,*
> *And Thou wert left alone,*
> *Every existence would exist in Thee.*"

It belonged to Charles Wesley when he wrote :

> " *Soul of my soul, remain !*
> *Who didst for all fulfil,*
> *In me, O Lord, fulfil again*
> *Thy heavenly Father's will !* "

It finds repeated expression in Tennyson :

> " *But that one ripple on the boundless deep*
> *Feels that the deep is boundless, and itself*
> *For ever changing form, but evermore*
> *One with the boundless motion of the deep.*"

He knew that there was a " knowledge " which was like

> " *the swallow on the lake*
> *That sees and stirs the surface-shadow there*
> *But never yet hath dipt into the abysm.*"

He who is " known " in true, deep knowledge is " the Nameless," in whom all things consist :

> " *And if the Nameless should withdraw from all*
> *Thy frailty counts most real, all thy world*
> *Might vanish like thy shadow in the dark.*"

He is " the Nameless," not because He is unknown, but because He is uncomprehended :

> " *Speak to Him thou for He hears, and Spirit with Spirit can meet :*
> *Closer is He than breathing, and nearer than hands and feet.*
> " *And the ear of man cannot hear, and the eye of man cannot see ;*
> *But if we could see and hear, this Vision —were it not He ?* "

Expressions such as these can be paralleled in many of the Fathers of the Church. Augustine in the *Confessions* speaks a different language from that which is heard in some of his other works. " When I call for Him I shall be calling Him into myself. . . . I should not be, O my God, I should not be at all if Thou wert not in me, or rather I should not be if I wert not in Thee, of whom all things, by whom all things, and in whom are all things." [1]   " And being thence admonished to return into myself, I entered even into my inward self, Thou being my guide ; and able I was, for Thou wert become my Helper. And I entered and beheld with the eye of my soul, above the same eye of my soul, above my mind, the Light Unchangeable." [2]

Hildebert sings, seeking to express the truth while excluding all possible errors :

> " *Super cuncta, subter cuncta ;*
> *Extra cuncta, intra cuncta ;*
> *Intra cuncta, nec inclusus ;*
> *Extra cuncta, nec exclusus ;*
> *Super cuncta, nec elatus ;*

[1] Bk. i., 2.   [2] Bk. vii., 10.

Subter cuncta, nec substratus ;
Super totus, praesidendo ;
Subter totus, sustinendo ;
Extra totus, complectendo ;
Intra totus es, implendo ;
Intra, nunquam coarctaris ;
Extra, nunquam dilataris ;
Super, nullo sustenaris ;
Subter, nullo fatigaris.
Mundum movens, non moveris,
Locum tenens, non teneris,
Tempus mutans, non mutaris,
Vaga firmans, non vagaris."

" Unless the Maker and Sustainer becomes also the indwelling Life and Mind and the inspiring Love," said F. H. Bradley, "how much of the Universe is impoverished ! . . . Banish all that is meant by the indwelling Spirit of God, in its harmony and discord with the finite soul, and what death and desolation has taken the place of living religion ! " [1]

All such emphases on the " Immanence " of God are in line with the statement of the Elohistic writer in Genesis i. 27 : " So God

[1] *Essays on Truth and Reality*, p. 437.

created man in his own image ; in the image of God created He him." The insight of all the seers of all the ages confirms this " doctrine " of " Immanence."

It is clear that all such utterances have a central affinity with the mind of the Johannine author. He who knew that the secret of Jesus was his unique communion with the Father would have understood every statement we have quoted. Probably the lines of Hildebert would have perplexed him. The endeavour to state a truth, while at the same time excluding every conceivable " error " of interpretation, was not his way of writing. His mind did not work that way. Enough for him to have understood the meaning of all spiritual religion. Enough for him to have found this meaning " incarnated " in Jesus. To others he left the task of excluding all the possible " errors "—with also, alas, the possibility of excluding in the endeavour the essential truth. The " Incarnation " he saw and proclaimed rested upon the " Immanence " for which religion stands. When, later on, the Church endeavoured to make this " religious immanence " fit into a scheme of thought to which God was in " substance " wholly distinct from man, the result was an inevitable " incoherence." The *presuppositions* of the Christological statements were not the *religious* significance of Jesus, but *ontological* theories with which somehow or another that had to be fused. The " fusion " becomes an Absorption, and the absorption becomes a disappearance. Religion has been swallowed by an ontological dualism, and we look in vain for the unity of the personal life of the Jesus of the Gospels.

The suggestion I have here made is that we shall never begin to approach an adequate statement of " the Historic Incarnation " until we have determined to refuse to relegate the utterances of the religious consciousness to a place subsidiary to a rationalistic metaphysic. The trouble is that in the heart of a good deal of theology there is a deep-seated antipathy to this method of approach. I believe it dominates many recent interpreters of this Gospel, who are, otherwise, critical of the traditional method of approach to Christology. Failing to see the *religious* key to the interpretation of the Gospel, or being unable to believe that this *can be* a key, they regard the Gospel as dominated and controlled by abstract theological ideas.[1] What I have suggested is that detail of precise historicity is dominated and controlled by the *real history*, and this real history is nothing less than the religious consciousness of Jesus. The writer had not perceived God at the end of a metaphysical telescope, if I may venture a phrase which will be understood by those who have pondered Lalande's famous remark. He had seen God " in the face of Jesus Christ." He had not *inferred* the Love of God from the perplexing facts of Nature and of History. These enigmatic facts only lose the desolating nature of their perplexity when they are seen in the light of a Faith which is not a demonstration but an insight. Then they are *accepted*, and not juggled with. " God," said our author, " is Love " (1 Jn. iv. 8). And he knew this because it flowed out of the whole fact of Jesus ; and he could not have seen this fact unless there had been *rapport*

[1] Cf. the view of E. F. Scott : " the history is everywhere subordinated to abstract, theological ideas " (*Literature of the New Testament*, p. 242).

between his own mind and the eternal in Jesus.

Let us consider, for example, that passage from the Gospel which is frequently regarded as the greatest " text " in the Scriptures, and as containing the core of Christianity. I refer to John iii. 16: " God so loved the world that He gave His only Son, that whosoever believeth on him may, instead of perishing, have eternal Life." This saying I take to be a dramatic declaration of the essential consciousness and experience of Jesus. He, whose own direct consciousness of God, whose own assured insight into the Divine Nature, enabled him to say " Father," *knew* that God was *Love*—Holy Love. All was of Divine Grace, all was given in Love. Love always gives. It is Love's prerogative. It is, further, our human test of Love. Jesus was conscious that his knowledge of the Father was *given*. Though he " learned obedience," and though " obedience " led him to an ever-deepening knowledge of the Father's Will, yet this knowledge was not, to him, *earned :* it was *given*. This sense of complete dependence on the Father throbs through the whole evangelical narrative : it belongs to the deepest consciousness of the historic Jesus. " Dependence " is the human side of " Grace." And so it is true to that consciousness to say that Jesus knew himself *given* by the Father for His other children, wandering and lost children, in order that they too might enter into the life abundant, the life that was life indeed.

This is what the Johannine author says in this great, and essentially true, utterance. God has given Jesus, the unique outpouring of His Love, and those who have " believed on him "—not given assent to a dogma about him, but with trustful insight have accepted him as the Father's Word and Deed—have found, here in time and place, the life that is " eternal."

The Johannine author would have understood what Thomas Heywood was saying when he wrote :

> " *I ask't the seas, and all the deep below,*
> *My God to know.*
> *I ask't the reptiles, and whatever is*
> *In the abysse ;*

Even from the shrimpe to the leviathan
Enquiry ran;
But in those deserts which no line can
*   sound*
The God I sought for was not to be found."

Such an inquiry will be for ever vain unless
it is illumined by the light within which flows
from Him who dwelleth in light unapproach-
able and full of glory. Those who are thus
illumined are able to understand the word,
" My Father worketh until now, and I work "
(Jn. v. 17). We shall never find God in the
universe without until we have known Him
in the universe within. This is not a philosophy which perpetuates " the insoluble
conflict of head and heart." It is the
" philosophy " which gives meaning to that
conflict ; it makes it " soluble " in the only
way that the inherent greatness and eternity
of life renders possible.

The philosophy, and ultimate " metaphysic," is seen when it is noted that the
Johannine position rests, not upon our human
love for God, but upon the objective fact of
the Love *of God*. " Love," he says, " is *of*
God " (1 Jn. iv. 7). " We love Him because

He first loved us " (1 Jn. iv. 19). "No man hath beheld God at any time; if we love one another, God abideth in us, and His love is perfected in us" (1 Jn. iv. 12). There is the Prevenient Light which is the source of all true human seeking, and the Prevenient Love which is the basis of all true human harmony. This is the vital kernel of any Christian doctrine of "Grace." The desperate theological encounters which this "doctrine" has witnessed through the centuries were only possible because the Johannine emphasis had been obscured. Again the "fusion" became an absorption, and the absorption became a disappearance.

"It is not wisdom to be only wise,
And on the inward vision close the eyes."

The Johannine author bids us return, not to a dogma of Grace, but to the experience of Grace whence all doctrines spring. It is an insight which sees what Grace is, not a statement which declares what we think it ought to mean. When Augustine had entered into his inmost self, as he tells us in the passage from the *Confessions* already quoted, and with the

eye of his soul had beheld above the same
eye of his soul and of his mind the Light
Unchangeable, he went on to say : "He
who knows the Truth, knows what that Light
is ; and he who knows it, knows eternity.
Love knoweth it. O Truth Who art Eternity !
and Love Who art Truth ! and Eternity Who
art Love ! Thou art my God." [1]

Thus there is in the Johannine " mysticism "
a true basis for a " Christian Doctrine of God."
It is not an insight which rejoices in itself,
or glories in its self-sufficiency. More, and
with deeper meaning, than any modern " dialectic" theologian, it can say, "To God
alone the Glory." For there is no Glory of
God which is not a *Self*-manifestation ; and
there is no Self-*manifestation* unless we can
recognise It when we see It ; and to recognise
It when we see It means the Immanent
Prevenience of God. It is in this Light that
we see light. Without this basis the modern
tension between head and heart will never
be resolved. Without it we work with " transcendence " and "immanence" like counters
in a clever game of dialectic. " I then being

[1] Bk. vii. 10.

thus gross-hearted," if I may quote Augustine again, " nor clear even to myself, whatsoever was not extended over certain spaces, nor diffused, nor condensed, nor swelled out, or did not or could not receive some of these dimensions, I thought to be altogether nothing. For over such forms as my eyes are wont to range, did my heart then range : nor yet did I see that this same motion of the mind, whereby I formed those very images, was not of this sort, and yet it could not have formed them, had not itself been some great thing. So also did I endeavour to conceive of Thee, Life of my Life, as vast, through infinite spaces, on every side penetrating the whole mass of the universe, and beyond it, every way, through unmeasurable boundless spaces ; so that the earth should have Thee, the heaven have Thee, all things have Thee, and they be bounded in Thee, and Thou bounded nowhere. . . . So I guessed, only as unable to conceive aught else, for it was false. For thus should a greater part of the earth contain a greater portion of Thee, and a less, a lesser ; and all things should in such part be full of Thee, that the body of an elephant should contain more of Thee than that of a sparrow, by how much larger it is, and takes up more room ; and thus shouldest Thou make the several portions of the world, in fragments, large to the large, petty to the petty. *But such art not Thou.*" [1]

The " subjectivism " from which " dialectic " theology seeks to deliver the age, is not escaped by dogmatic assertions that there is a " word of God " apart from all our seeing. We cannot say that something is there if we do not see it, however determined the dogmatic iterations and reiterations. There is a " subjectivism " in the very heart of all personal life, and the only way to escape it is by seeing its significance. We do not escape it by denying that it is there, or by conceiving of God as treating it as if it were not there. The very denial of it is an unmistakable assertion of it. Neither religion nor thinking can ever rest on the denial of the Descartian " Cogito ergo sum." In a lecture delivered some time ago on the " dialectic theology " by one of its supporters the following argument against " subjectivity "

[1] *Confessions*, Bk. vii. 1.

in religion was used. I give the precise words used, according to the verbatim report : " To arrive at certainty about God's existence by referring to men's aspirations toward Him is as impossible as to convince a thirsty traveller in the desert that there must be an oasis quite near because he is so thirsty." It never seemed to have struck the speaker that the traveller would never have known what thirst was if there had been no such thing as water. Thirst presupposes water to quench it. To *assert* dogmatically the " certainty " of God's existence to anyone who has no aspiration after him is like bringing a draught of water to a traveller who has died of thirst. It is only as we have experience of God that we can know either that He exists or what His nature is. In our aspiration is our seeing, and in our seeing is our aspiration. To deny the immanental vision of religious experience in the interests of a dogma *about* transcendence is like plucking out one's eyes in order to see better. Even Transcendence is only known when we see it. There is no profounder misreading of Christian " mysticism " than to imagine that it takes refuge in itself, or is centred in itself. It is centred upon the Objective Reality of God, who is known in experience. Such a misreading would seem to spring from the devastating scepticism that the Reality of God cannot be known in human experience. To such a scepticism no dogmatic affirmations such as characterise a good deal of what is now frequently called " the Barthian challenge to religious experience " will avail to bring certainty. These dogmatic affirmations spring from a deeper doubt than any they can ever answer—they spring from the doubt that man cannot by the constitution of his own spiritual, moral and rational nature come to know God. To such a doubt it is clearly futile to declare— " Here at this specific point, in this specific ' Word,' God speaks : therefore, submit, obey." It is futile, because on the fundamental hypothesis we cannot hear Him when He speaks, we cannot know Him when He reveals Himself. We do not achieve " objectivity " in religion by declaring that man can never *know* God : what we achieve is complete nescience. Any theology which begins by denying the bond which unites God and man condemns itself to a perpetual inability to say anything about the Transcendent who is the object of religion. Of the Transcendence which denies the very vision which affirms It, we must say : *But such art not Thou.*

Nor is the " subjectivity " of the Johannine religious insight just a vague doctrine of " the inner light." This " inner light " has had its unique manifestation in that light which is " the light of the knowledge of the glory of God in the face of Jesus Christ." The message of Johannine " mysticism " is inseparably linked to the historical, as we have sought already to show. When George Fox said that " though he read of Christ and God, he knew them only from a like spirit in his own soul," he was saying nothing which is not said, with another accent, in the New Testament. But he did not always remember his indebtedness to History for his own personal insight which had been mediated to him from all the past. This the Johannine author never forgot. " The light which lighteth every man coming into the world " was the light whose incarnate glory he had beheld in the life of Jesus Christ. God who is " Spirit," and who

must be worshipped " in spirit and in truth,"
is " Father," and he who has seen Jesus has
seen the Father (Jn. xiv. 9). The Spirit,
that was to Wordsworth

> " *Spirit that knows no insulated spot,*
> *No chasm, no solitude ; from link to link*
> *It circulates, the Soul of all the worlds* "—

that Spirit had been seen in time and place.
It is thus that the Johannine author makes
the emphasis on history to cohere with the
emphasis on the " inner light " of religious
experience. He at least did not teach what
Pfleiderer called " the fatal ban of historicism,
which seeks God's revelation only in the records of a dead past and thus loses its power
of finding it in the living present." [1] To him
there was a *fruitful* historicism, which recognises in the facts of history the source and
the inspiration of the capacity to discover
God's revelation in each successive age. And
the most fruitful fact of history for him and
for the Christian thinker is in the fact of Jesus
himself. In this connection, it is significant
that in the context where Jesus says that the

[1] *Early Christian Conception of Christ,* p. 170.

Spirit will guide his disciples into all the truth he goes on to add : " He shall glorify me : for he shall take of mine, and shall declare it unto you" (xvi. 13, 14). To the Johannine author, it is the light that shone in Jesus that guides wayfarers into " the increasing truth."

The Johannine emphasis, therefore, enables us to hold together the two essential elements in Christianity—the *historical* and the *eternal*. The historical has significance as seen in the light of the eternal, and the eternal is ours in the depth of our personal life, and uniquely " incarnate " in Jesus, the Christ.

(III) *The Message about Man.*—I wish to show, in the third place, that the Johannine emphasis, as I have sought here to interpret it, involves a profound and, as I hold, the only really satisfying and satisfactory doctrine of man. In the previous sections I have sought to show that in this Johannine emphasis there is a message about God and a message about the place and significance of Jesus in Christianity. For a full-orbed message, however, Christianity must have something to say about man. We have here a great trinity in unity. *God*, the fount of all reality and of all value : *the historic Jesus*, to whom our supreme and unforgettable indebtedness is due for the manifestation of God which has shone forth from the depths of his personal life here in time and place : *man himself*, whose worth and meaning are clearly revealed in the light of God thus manifest.

It is obvious that the " immanence " given us in the whole depth of man's religious experience of God involves a doctrine of man. The claim that God may be really " known " within and through the complete personal life of man necessarily rests upon the truth that man is a being transcending the limitations of time and space. To " know " God ! What a claim is this ! Even the very claim to have such " knowledge " is an out-reaching of the spirit of man beyond the mere physical environment belonging to sense-perceptions. There is only one satisfactory thing to say about this out-reaching of man's being, and that is, that it belongs to the very *essence* of his nature. To say that man does this in order to deceive himself as to the intrinsic unmeaningness of life, or in order to gratify desires for a life which never can be his, is a specious and facile answer which has run away from the real problem. For the question still remains, why, if there be no real meaning in personal life, man, who has this life, should ever even begin to conceive of an environment of spiritual reality transcending the only reality which, according to the hypothesis, exists. I believe that if this question be pondered it will be seen that *meaning* is integral to the very fact of personal life. To conceive, on the *illusion* hypothesis, that man creates something that isn't there, in order to satisfy selfish desires of his being, is to leave the question altogether unfaced as to the fact that he has at least *created* something transcending all he is supposed to know about. Which shows, I would submit, that he knows about more than he is supposed to know about : in other words, that there is more in reality than has been, on the sceptical hypothesis, held to exist. This plea may also be brought to the consideration of the *sociological* illusionists, of whom M. Durkheim was the distinguished father.

The spiritual *capacity* of man points to a spiritual universe that is there. The religious experience of man is the Divine self-manifestation. Reality is known, not by what, in scientific theory, man has developed *from*, but by what he has developed *to*. The God who is the Father of our spirits is known to us because we have been made in His image, after His likeness.

The position here taken is that religious experience means divine immanence, and divine immanence means some eternal value in man. Nor is this mere circular argumentation. We

are not in the realm where logical demonstration is possible. To say that the position,
therefore, is mere arguing in a circle is to take
a logical standing-ground from which to rebut
a statement on spiritual reality which, as
I have sought to maintain, transcends the
categories of logic. The true rationality of
the position is that it gives meaning to life
and to the universe. In the very nature of
the case no other, and lower, form of rationality
is possible.

It will be seen that the position is far removed from the creed known as " pantheism."
There is a " Higher Pantheism " belonging
to all religious insight ; but it is poles asunder
from the abstract pantheism wherein God,
the Supreme Personal Self, and the personal
self of man, alike disappear in a universal
" It." The " pantheism " which loses the
significance of the personal relation between
God and man has obviously no affinity with
that doctrine of divine immanence which flows
out of that personal relation known in the
religious consciousness. To say that man in
the depths of his whole personal life *knows*
God is the very negation of the position that

the river of man's personal life is merged in the ocean of the impersonal Absolute. The river knows not the ocean, nor does the ocean know the river. Such a figure of speech as the river and the ocean—so familiar to pantheistic thought—rests upon a mere *abstract* foundation, and involves, as it has always seemed to me, the negation of the personal values by which it has been constructed. Both he who knows and He who is known are merged in an Unknowing and Unknowable Absolute. Such a creed is not only inadequate to personal religion, but is its complete negation. God is neither "external" to our spirits, nor is He "coincident," or "identical," with them. These are both spatial metaphors, whose inadequacy will be seen by the most superficial observer. To live with God is not to be indistinguishable from God. To know Him is to know that He is the Immanent, transcending our spirits. A Christian doctrine of immanence never identifies man with God. Throbbing through the doctrine is the sense of Dependence, of Claim, of Ought, of Grace. Browning spoke of one aspect of this when, in *A Death in the Desert*, he wrote :

> " *Man is not God, but hath God's end to
>   serve,*
> *A Master to obey, a course to take,*
> *Somewhat to cast off, somewhat to become.*"

And in his *Christmas Eve* he gave classical
expression to a Christian doctrine of man :

> " *Take all in a word : the truth in God's
>   breast*
> *Lies trace for trace upon ours impressed :*
> *Though He is so bright and we so dim,*
> *We are made in His image to witness
>   Him.*"

It is highly significant, and also, as I suggest,
truly coherent with the main line of thought
throughout these pages, that the Fourth
Gospel, which so directly penetrates to the
inner truth of the nature of Jesus, also sets
forth the truth that the essence of every man's
nature lies in his ethical and spiritual relationship to God.   The Gospel is no more concerned
with a carefully elaborated and fully thought-
out theology of man than it is with a precise Christology.   The intricate, speculative
problems with which the Church's thinkers
were later concerned—Creationism and Tra-

ducianism, Pelagianism, Semi-Pelagianism and Augustianism, and kindred issues—were not, I believe, in the orbit of the author's thought. Here, too, his interest was religious and not metaphysical, experiential and not speculative. And the significant thing to note is that throughout the Gospel there are passages which indicate that the relationship which *ought* to exist between men and God is analogous to the relationship which *did* exist between Jesus and God. In passing I would suggest that in this fact there is additional substantiation for the conclusion already drawn—namely, that we must not attribute to the author of the Gospel what is called the conception of the " metaphysical sonship " of Jesus. As, indeed, we shall not attribute to his mind a doctrine of the " metaphysical sonship " of other men. All such modes of interpretation founder on the rock of a *religious* interpretation of the Gospel. As little should we attribute to his mind a speculative theory of the " metaphysical sonship " of *some* men, as we should attribute to him a speculative theory of some kind of " metaphysical sonship " from " the devil " of some

204 THE FOURTH GOSPEL

other men. Let me illustrate from the Gospel
what this precisely means.

In the Gospel Jesus declares that His disciples were not of this world, even as he was
not of this world (see Jn. xvii. 14, 16 ; also
xv. 19 ; 1 Jn. iv. 4 ff.). Here, is he not speaking of real spiritual fellowship to be sought
and enjoyed by his disciples, a fellowship
analogous to that perfect fellowship which he
knew ? In these same discourses Jesus prays
for his disciples " that they may all be one ;
even as Thou, Father, art in me, and I in Thee,
that they also may be in us " (xvii. 21).
He also prays that the love wherewith the
Father loved him may be in the disciples,
and he in them (xvii. 26). Here again,
the thought moves on the plane of spiritual
and ethical fellowship, not of " metaphysical
union." Jesus, who to the Johannine author
is " the Word," says in this Gospel : " He
that is of God heareth *the words* of God "
(viii. 47). Does not this mean that a fellowship, in some true measure analogous to that
which belonged in a unique degree to Jesus,
may be known to others who also hear the
voice of God ? He who is the unique mani-

festation, "incarnation," of the "Word"
says that his brethren may enjoy the spiritual
communion with the Father which the term
"Word" itself betokens. And in the same
passage Jesus is declared as saying that his
adversaries are not of God because they do
not hear these words of God (viii. 47).
The meaning surely is that they are not in
harmonious spiritual union with God ; they
therefore do not hear the words of one who
is. They do not hear and believe his words
because they are not of his sheep (x. 26)
And so Jesus declares in this Gospel that
these adversaries of his have sprung from
their father, the devil, as he is sprung from
God, his Father (viii. 42-44). If we understand the spiritual interpretation of the
Gospel, we shall perceive that here the writer
is not setting forth a speculative theory of
a physical, or metaphysical, origin of some
men from "the devil" ; he is referring to
the whole ethical and spiritual orientation of
their personality. He is concerned with the
experienced fact of what they were, not with
the speculative question as to whence they had
the origin of their being. It is thus that we

shall penetrate to the meaning of these con-
troversial, or polemical, passages in the Gospel.
Jesus speaks the things which he has heard
from his Father, as they also speak and do
the things they have heard from their father
(viii. 38). In spite of the fact that these
his adversaries have the Old Testament
Scriptures, in spite even of the fact that they
have searched them, they have not heard the
voice of God, for God's *word* does not abide
in them ; and so they do not see and hear
Jesus who is come in the Father's name, and
is indeed His very " Word " (v. 37 ff.).

In accordance with this whole method of
interpretation, we see the meaning of all
such passages where the disciples of Jesus are
regarded as the peculiar objects of the Divine
love, as he himself is. The love that binds
him to the Father is the love that binds
them to himself. This love is a virtual
" abode " of the Father and himself with
the disciples (xiv. 21, 23-4 ; xvi. 27 ; xvii.
26). He prays that the spiritual and ethical
fellowship of mutual love which he has with
the Father may constitute the very " unity "
of his disciples. The same expression is used

to indicate both "unions" (εἶναι ἕν, xvii. 11, 21, 22). What a commentary on the degeneracies which the materialistic mind of the Church has brought to New Testament conceptions is found in the institutionalised interpretations of the Church's "Unity" which have pervaded so much of the Church's thought![1]

It is obvious, therefore, that what has been called "the doctrine of man" in the Fourth Gospel is not so much a "doctrine" as an insight, and a "message." It is the insight which declares that man is so constituted that he can hold ethical and spiritual fellowship with God. It is the very prerogative of his being that he may be "a son of God." In this teaching the Fourth Gospel, let it be said in passing, is again in line with the Synoptic Gospels. For there it is as love fills the life that men become sons of the Father

[1] The "other sheep" passage has been similarly subject to crude ecclesiastical interpretations. All have to be gathered into one compact organisation! This is held to be the "one *fold*," about which Jesus speaks in Jn. x. 16, where it is conveniently overlooked that the word is "*flock*" not "fold." Well may the question be asked as to whether degeneration could further go.

who is in heaven (Matt. v. 44-45). But what is stressed is the experienced fact of man's fellowship with God, not the speculative question as to his "origin." Nevertheless, the fact that such an experience is possible to man indicates the exceeding high view of man's nature as taught by Jesus. He to whom God can speak and make Himself known must have, dare we not say, some essential kinship of nature with God. Such a truth is "given" in the very fact of man's communion with God. When the developing child looks up into his father's face and reads the meaning of both the approving smile and the condemning frown he knows what it is to be a true "son." It is not physical paternity that makes him a "son," but the inward fellowship whereby he "knows" his father's heart and mind. And such a fellowship is only possible in so far as the "son" partakes in some measure of that same nature which constitutes the essential being of the father. "Behold," says the Johannine author in his first Epistle, "what manner of love the Father hath bestowed upon us, that we should be called children of God : and such we are "

(iii. 1). While, therefore, to the Johannine author, as to Jesus himself, "sonship" does not involve a thought-out philosophy of origination, it does involve an essential community of nature. And while he would, as I believe, have been perplexed by the later discussions on "substantiality" and "consubstantiality," he would have known what a modern writer—Professor Radhakrishnan—*means* when he says : "The consubstantiality of the spirit in man and God is the conviction fundamental to all spiritual wisdom." [1]

"God is light and in him is no darkness at all," says our author (1 Jn. i. 5). Elsewhere he says : "Believe on the light, that ye may become sons of light" (Jn. xii. 36). To say that men may become "sons of light" means the same as to say that they may become "sons of God." To "believe on the light" is to believe on the name of Jesus, in whom the fullness of the light dwells, who is, indeed, "the light of the world." For he says, "As many as receiveth him, he gave to them the right to become children of God, to those believing on his name" (Jn. i. 12).

[1] *An Idealist Interpretation of Life*, p. 103.

When Judas was completely alienated from the mind and purposes of Jesus, he went out into " the night " (Jn. xiii. 30). " Darkness " to the writer, is to be out of harmony with God. It belongs to " the world " with its transience, in contrast with that ethical harmony with God wherein consists the life that is eternal. " Love not the world, neither the things that are in the world. If any man love the world, the love of the Father is not in him. For all that is in the world, the lust of the flesh, and the lust of the eyes, and the vainglory of life, is not of the Father, but is of the world. And the world passeth away, and the lust thereof : but he that doeth the will of God abideth for ever " (1 Jn. ii. 15-17).

To the author, therefore, " sin " is not some great abstract entity, to be discussed as a thing in and by itself. He is not concerned with the metaphysical question as to its " origin " : he is concerned with it as a reality of human experience. We look in vain in his writings for soteriological theories which are built upon the " necessity " of a " death " which, so, will remove this entity and make it possible for God to do what otherwise He

could not, or would not, do. Sin is the
darkness of moral disobedience to God in
the concrete minds of men. It is not something men "inherit"; it is something they
manifest in their lives. Men's works are
"evil" when they love "darkness" instead
of the "light" (Jn. iii. 19). "For every one
that doeth ill hateth the light, and cometh
not to the light, lest his works should be
reproved. But he that doeth the truth
cometh to the light, that his works may be
made manifest, that they have been wrought
in God" (iii. 20-1). Sin is a "bondage"
(viii. 34), and freedom comes to men when
they "know the truth," which is "incarnate"
in Jesus. "Ye shall know the truth, and
the truth shall make you free": "If therefore
the Son shall make you free, ye shall be free
indeed" (viii. 32 and 36). "Truth" to Jesus
is not conceived in a mere intellectualist
manner; it is the manifestation of the spiritual
and ethical reality that is God. "'What is
truth,' said jesting Pilate; and would not
stay for an answer."[1] To Jesus, and the
author of this Gospel, "truth" is seen wherever

[1] See Bacon's Essay "Of Truth."

ethical and spiritual reality is revealed.   And
so in the Gospel Jesus says to Pilate : " To
this end have I been born, and to this end
am I come into the world, that I should bear
witness unto the truth. Every one that is
of the truth heareth my voice " (xviii.
37-8). Sin is not, therefore, just ignorance—
that is, it is not a mere intellectual quality
or deficiency : it is the volition of the whole
personal nature. So to the Pharisees Jesus
says : " If ye were blind, ye would have
no sin ; but now ye say, We see : your sin
remaineth " (ix. 41). It is not mere acquiescence in darkness ; it is a positive hatred of
light (iii. 20). And so " the world " hateth
Jesus, because he testifies of it, that its works
are evil (vii. 7). It is because his disciples
are not of " this world " that it hates them
(xv. 19). " Marvel not, brethren, if the
world hateth you. We know that we have
passed out of death into life, because we love
the brethren. He that loveth not abideth in
death. Whosoever hateth his brother is a
murderer : and ye know that no murderer
hath eternal life abiding in him " (1 Jn. iii.
13-15). " He that saith he is in the light,

and hateth his brother, is in the darkness even until now. He that loveth his brother abideth in the light, and there is none occasion of stumbling in him " (1 Jn. ii. 9-10). " If a man say, I love God, and hateth his brother, he is a liar : for he that loveth not his brother whom he hath seen, cannot love God whom he hath not seen " (1 Jn. iv. 20).

In all such passages from the Johannine writings we have a strong ethical message—undying in its penetration. Here there is an insight beyond which mankind will never go. It is eternal, as is the ethical nature of God Himself, on which the message is grounded. His message is not just " Let us be good " : it is " Let us love one another, for love is of God " (1 Jn. iv. 7). " God is love " (1 Jn. iv. 8). For man to love is not to screw himself up in order to do something foreign to his true nature : it is for him to manifest the very nature of the Divine which belongs to his essential being. And, to the writer, it is because Jesus so perfectly manifested this love in his life that he is uniquely God's Son. His death on the Cross reveals the depth and intensity of this love, and the disciples are exhorted to be like him in such a love. " This is my commandment, That ye love one another, as I have loved you. Greater love hath no man than this, that he lay down his life for his friends " (xv. 12-13) —this, significantly enough, was one of the favourite texts of Abelard. Therefore, when a Christian looks on the Cross, he can say, if he has the Johannine insight which derives from Jesus himself : " God is like that." And when he says that, he does not mean that the Cross is the evidence of a propitiatory theory of Atonement : he means that the truest thing man can say about God is that He is perfect, holy love, for here in the Cross it has its sublimest manifestation.[1]   The glory

[1] The well-known passage in the first Epistle of John (1 Jn. ii. 2) is often quoted to rebut this interpretation of the author's view of the Cross : " he is the ἱλασμός (' propitiation ') for our sins." But the one certain fact about the exegesis of this passage is that our word " propitiation " is not an adequate translation of ἱλασμός : in other words, there is no thought that Christ propitiates God. The thought of the author is that Christ is the Divine manifestation of mercy vouchsafed to sinful men, and not the means by which that mercy can be secured. The substantive is cognate to the verb used by the publican in his prayer for Divine mercy in Luke xviii. 13—ἱλάσθητι μοι, " be merciful unto me." The same word ἱλασμός is also used in 1 Jn. iv. 10.

of the Cross is that it is the self-offering of
Jesus in perfect love. The writer derives
from Jesus himself the strong note of ethical
volition. He is not concerned with the
speculative questions of a " metaphysical
necessity " for the death of Jesus. " The Son "
could have refused the Cross ; all that was
necessary was that he should repudiate his
values, and so abandon his whole purpose
of bringing the life of eternal blessedness to
men. But to do this was to cease to be
himself. " Therefore doth the Father love
me, because I lay down my life, that I may
take it again. No one taketh it away from
me, but I lay it down of myself. I have
power to lay it down, and I have power to
take it again. This commandment I received
from my Father " (x. 17-18). Here there is
no " un-morality " of acquiescence in inevitable
destiny ; there is, rather, an unswerving
fidelity to the Divine nature that was his.
The Cross is " Divine " because it manifests
the essential " Divinity " of a perfect, self-
offering love. Its " necessity " arises from
the spiritual insight and ethical sublimity of
the personality of Jesus. It is this that

constitutes him the " Word " of the Father.
To say that the death of Jesus on the Cross
was " God's will for him " means this—no less,
and no more. I say " no less," for it was not
" the accidental fate of goodness in conflict
with evil," not merely " the natural fruit
of Jewish bigotry and Roman indifference."
It could only be such a " fruit " in so far as
Jesus himself gave himself, voluntarily, to a
life of conflict with all the darkness and
evil of men, a life of perfect obedience to the
Father. I say " no more," for the concern
and interest of Jesus in the Gospel is not with
the speculative questions of " predestination,"
but with the experienced fact of his knowledge of the Father's will. It was the Father's
will that he should be true to the vision of
life which had been granted him, true to the
knowledge of God he had, true to the direct
communion with the Father which was his.
It could never be " the Father's will " that he
should lower the flag, surrender to the calls
of worldly expediency, refuse to be his own
true, holy self. It could never be the Father's
will that he should exploit the political, the
dogmatic, the ecclesiastical frailties of his
countrymen.

I have referred to this Johannine message of the Cross at this point because of its harmony with the whole spiritual and ethical emphasis of the Gospel. This is no treatise on Soteriology, and I do not discuss the death of Jesus from that point of view. What I have been seeking in this section to maintain is that the spiritual and ethical nature of man means a partaking of the Divine nature. And the Cross of the man Jesus exemplifies more clearly than any other incident in the Gospel that community of spiritual and ethical nature. Herein he, " the first-born of many brethren," reveals his " consubstantiality " of nature with that of God. His message to men is to be true to the Divine nature of their own real selves. They also are to take up the cross, and so follow him. It is when he tells his disciples that his complete dedication to the will of God is to lead him to Jerusalem that he enunciates the same principle as binding for them as well. " If any man would come after me, let him deny himself, and take up his cross and follow me. For whosoever would save his life shall lose it ; and who-

soever shall lose his life for my sake shall
find it" (Matt. xvi. 24-5). In the Fourth
Gospel we find the same association. At the
last feast in Jerusalem, when certain Greeks
come seeking him, Jesus declares that the
principle of dying-to-live, which he has embraced, must also be embraced by those who
would be his disciples. "Except a grain of
wheat fall into the ground and die, it abideth
by itself alone ; but if it die, it beareth much
fruit. He that loveth his life loseth it ; and
he that hateth his life in this world shall
keep it unto life eternal" (xii. 24-5). This,
to use the words of Milton in *Comus*, is

> "*that golden key*
> *That opes the palace of eternity.*"

The Cross of Jesus was the final and conclusive manifestation of the principle which
governed his whole life ; and it is the same
truly Divine principle which he calls his disciples to exhibit in their lives. It is this
culminating manifestation of his whole spirit
in the Cross which is to draw all men to the
recognition of its divinity. "I if I be lifted
up from the earth, will draw all men unto

myself" (xii. 32). It is here, if I may use
the words, that men come to awake to the
" consubstantiality " of their true nature with
that of God. It is here, by the piercing of
our darkness by the light which gleams from
the Cross, that we may emerge into the light
of a conscious unity with God.

The message of the Johannine Gospel, as of
the Synoptic Gospels, is that the *Gospel of God*
is a *Gospel of man*. When I say that it is a
Gospel of God I mean that it is all grounded
in the nature of God Himself : it is God's
self-manifestation, it is God's act, it is God's
will. There can be, as I have already said,
no real Gospel which is not a Gospel *of* God,
and a Gospel *about* God. Right from the Prologue this theocentric emphasis belongs to
the fourth evangelist. When I say that it is
a *Gospel of man* I mean that this Gospel of
God is a revelation of His will for man. The
manifestation of the Divine will, thought, and
essential nature in the " Word," exhibits
what man ought to be, and may become.
To sunder the divine from the human in Jesus
is not only to dissolve the unity of his personal
life—a unity which I must regard as axiomatic

—it is also to leave the Divine Gospel *of man* without any standing-ground of hope for the possibility of its consummation. It is here that the Johannine message of the Incarnation, as distinguished from the dogmatic formulations of Incarnation doctrine, shows the validity of this hope. Man may become what it is the Divine will he should become, because he can hear the Divine voice and know the Divine presence—because, in other words, he has kinship of nature with God. How could he become perfect even as his Father which is in heaven is perfect if eternity had not been set in his very nature ? How could he take Jesus as his supreme exemplar if Jesus did not reveal what human nature essentially is and what, therefore, it is in men to become ? How could the Divine " Grace "—which is the outflowing and manifestation of the Divine nature—ever " save " any man if there were not, in spite of his creaturely limitations and all the " darkness " of his sin, the capacity in his own nature to see what was manifested and to receive what was offered ?

The *doctrine of Divine Grace* necessarily

involves a lofty *doctrine of man*. The offering
of the Divine Grace is not, and by the very
nature of the case cannot be, the offering of
a static and inanimate *thing* to a static and
inanimate automaton. It is the offering of
the dynamic Divine nature to a being whose
own nature enables him to receive it and
co-operate with its purpose. A father's real
gifts can be only given to a " son." To one
who has less than the nature of " son " they
could never be " given," but only " imposed."
And a Divine " imposition " would destroy
both the ethical and spiritual nature of God
and the ethical and spiritual nature of man.
I can only give my child my love if he can
receive it. I can only dare to offer him
" forgiveness " if he is able to appropriate it.
These are gifts of the essential nature, and
presuppose in their receiver a kinship in this
nature. I can withhold a whipping from
my dog, when he has been disobedient—but
that is not the offering, and receiving, of a
forgiving love. I can only offer the *forgiveness
of love* to one who in some measure sees what
I see, feels what I feel, seeks what I seek. The
Christian doctrine of forgiveness is not a

doctrine of materialistic magic ; it is the doctrine of a Father's Grace to His own sons in their darkness and frailty and disobedience. It is of quality, not of quantity ; of life, not of death. We do a terrible disservice to religion if we conceive of it as a withholding of punishment, or as a magical impartation. A " salvation " which is independent of the spiritual insight and moral response of the receiver is no Christian doctrine. A mere passive reception involves the denial of the moral and spiritual nature of the receiver, and, further, degrades the very nature of the gift. I can pour water into a basin ; but I cannot pour grace into my son. To regard the Divine impartation of grace in any such *ex opere operato* manner is to degrade the grace and to destroy the " person " receiving it.

So frequently, the absolutely central Christian doctrine of Divine Grace is set, like a diamond, against the dull foil of a low and degrading doctrine of man. It seems to be felt by many that the best way to make God's Grace everything is to make man nothing. The scintillating stone, it is said, shines

most brightly against the dull platinum. The
figure, like all others, is inadequate, and we
can take out of it just what we wish to see
and to take. For myself, I would take out
of it an opposite message from that which
tormented and anguished shouting of " To
God alone the glory" seeks to derive. The
platinum is a good foil just because of its
value, and not just because of its dullness.
God is the Sole Giver ; but man is the *receiver*.
Every " gift " presupposes a receiver as well
as a giver. And the nature of the gift reveals
the nature both of the giver and of the receiver.
We do not show a high estimate of the value
of pearls by casting them before swine. Nor
do we show a high estimate of the value of
Divine Grace by regarding it as offered to
one who is less than worthy of it. Least of
all do we set it forth as having eternal value
when the conditions for its reception are less
than the loftiest spirituality and the deepest
morality. All the ecclesiastical " apologias "
for its safe and secure canalisation are, in
the end, a degrading of the " grace " which
is offered. The truest " catholicity " is one
that negates all human conceptions of " in-

stitutionalism." The deepest and worthiest
" sacramentalism " renders invalid the de-
based " sacramentalism " of necessary forms
and sacerdotal " successions." Whenever reception of the Divine Grace ceases to be spiri-
tually and ethically conditioned and becomes
ecclesiastically determined, corruption sets
in. Whenever the bonds which unite us to
God and to our fellows cease to be the bonds
of faith and of love they cease to be ties of
freedom. The bonds of ecclesiastical power
become the chains of servitude. It is *God's*
service alone that is perfect freedom.

I believe that an enlightened understanding
of the Johannine Gospel will reveal that the
Divine Grace is never conceived as bestowed
upon the inert and dully acquiescent. The
whole activity of the highest spirituality and
intensest morality is the human condition
for its reception. We must renounce to gain,
and die to live. The insight of faith is morally
conditioned. And so in the Nicodemus discourse we are told that the reason why men
rejected the light of the Divine Word was
because, *their works being evil,* they loved
darkness rather than the light (iii. 19).

" For every one that doeth ill hateth the light,
and cometh not to the light, lest his works
should be reproved : "—that is, exposed, recognised for what they were—" But he that
doeth the truth cometh to the light, that his
works may be made manifest, that they have
been wrought in God " (iii. 20-1). No cheap
or easy Gospel of man is here—and no morbid
and cloistered " mysticism "—no " salvation
by magic," whether soteriological or sacra-
mental magic. Those whose whole personality
is rightly oriented are led to the light : those
whose whole disposition is wrongly directed
are led to the darkness. And so in the
seventh chapter Jesus is declared as saying :
" The world hateth me, because I testify of it,
that its works are evil " (v. 7). And, in
the passage previously referred to, Jesus declares to Pilate that inasmuch as he is come
into the world to bear witness unto the truth,
every one who is of the truth hears his voice
(xviii. 37). In bearing witness to the truth,
Jesus does not seek his own glory. The acid
test of the *truth*-ful spirit is that it seeks the
glory of The All-Truthful and All-Righteous.
With this emphasis, Jesus conjoins that word

which has brought more peace to strong ethical souls than probably any other passage in the Gospels : " If any man willeth to do His will, he shall know of the teaching, whether it be of God " (vii. 17-18). In the same spirit, and with the same emphasis, Jesus is declared as saying to his Jewish adversaries who did not receive him : " How can ye believe, which receive glory of one another, and the glory that cometh from the only God ye seek not " (v. 44). The quest for the fleeting glory of men blinds to the eternal glory of God. The ignorance that is condemned is not the ignorance of lack of privilege but the ignorance of lack of will. The presence of any truth-loving man in a company of men reveals the lovers of truth and the lovers of falsehood : the self-seekers are always pugnaciously discomfited and hostilely abashed. Their inner discomfiture and abashment hides itself in a cloak of cunning and violent antipathy. The light does not come to make shadows, but yet makes them. Truth does not come to divide, but divides nevertheless. Love would embrace all, but is yet rejected by many. The Son loves, and would be loved by, all, but nevertheless encounters the hatred of hirelings. Knowing this, Jesus in his farewell address tells his disciples that as he has been persecuted so will they be. " A servant is not greater than his lord. If they persecuted me, they will also persecute you ; if they kept my word, they will keep yours also. But all these things will they do unto you for my name's sake, because they know not Him that sent me. If I had not come and spoken unto them, they had not had sin : but now they have no excuse for their sin " (xv. 20-2). The " sight " that prides itself on its narrow, earthly clarity, is of the blindness of sin. And so to the Pharisees, in another passage already referred to, Jesus says : " if ye were blind, ye would have no sin : but now ye say, We see : your sin remaineth " (ix. 41).

This whole emphasis on the paramount necessity, for the reception of the Divine Grace, of a right direction of the whole personality is in accord with all such Synoptic passages as those which tell us that Jesus came not to call the righteous but sinners to repentance, and with such a parable as that which contrasts the " righteous " Pharisee and the " unrighteous " publican. It is also harmonious with the firm universalistic note which is struck in the Johannine Gospel. " *Whosoever* believeth may in him have eternal life " (iii. 15). " God so loved the world " (iii. 16) ; Jesus, to the Samaritans, is " indeed the saviour of the world " (iv. 42 ; see also 1 Jn. iv. 14) ; Jesus is " the bread of life " which is given by the Father " unto the world " ; whoever comes to Jesus will neither hunger nor thirst—and yet there are many who will not come, there are many who will not eat—only those the Father gives to him will come and eat (vi. 33-7, 51). Jesus says that he is " the light of the world," and that whoever follows him will not walk in the darkness but will have the " light of life " ; yet the Pharisees will not see and will not follow (viii. 12 ff.). " I, if I be lifted up, will draw *all* men unto myself " ; yet many resist the inner constraint (xii. 32). He says : " I am come a light into the world, that whosoever believeth on me may not abide in the darkness " : yet there are those who reject him and receive not his sayings—these are

" judged " by the Divine word expressed by him (xii. 46-8). When all such passages are pondered in the setting of the inner meaning of the Gospel it will be seen that the universalistic note is fully harmonious with the conditioning note. The Gospel of man is a Gospel of what he *may*, and *ought to*, become : it is not a Gospel of what he, perforce, *must* become. God, who would have all men become " sons," treats them as such.

I am convinced that it is this lofty doctrine of man, running through the whole Johannine Gospel, which enables us to understand the polemical passages which occasion so much difficulty to many. It is, as I have earlier suggested, a dramatising polemic begotten of an insight into the essential significance of man. The dramatic genius of the author has overleapt itself, and so can be read, by those unsympathetic with his mind, as indicating an exclusiveness in the Gospel and spirit of Jesus. Such a reading of the Gospel, however, should be corrected by a reading of the Gospel in its entirety. The light shines upon all, but all do not see it. The very fierceness of these seemingly polemical passages springs from the overmastering insight that no man is saved in spite of himself, that the reception of the truth has its human conditions. These conditions are fulfilled in those who realise their own utter need ; they never can be fulfilled in those who are worldly-wise, in those who are self-seeking, in those who esteem cleverness above insight, in those who place " letter " before spirit, in those who are ecclesiastics before they are truthful men. All this, I am convinced, has come from Jesus himself, but it shines upon us in this Gospel, through a medium which distorts it because of the very intensity of the author's sympathy with it—a distortion which, doubtless, was also partly occasioned by the bitter polemical situation through which the Church had passed.

It will thus be seen by the reader that I do not regard this Gospel, with some recent interpreters, as representative of a narrow and exclusive ecclesiasticism. Such interpreters see in the Johannine author what I can only regard as a psychological self-contradiction. On the one hand is his sublime Christian universalism : on the other hand is his rigid

identification of Christianity with the ecclesiastical institution he knows. And so in his
Gospel the universalism is neutralised by the
ecclesiasticism : and the author becomes a man
whose deep Christian insight and feeling is
overlaid and rendered nugatory by the shallow,
narrow and pugnacious rigidity of the high
ecclesiastic. This I regard as an essential
misreading of the author's mind and of the
author's Gospel. It is a view dictated by
the theory that the Gospel is " an ecclesiastical
document," written in the interests of the
institution as such. Approached with this
presupposition the many universalistic passages are regarded as a relic of the spirit and
teaching of Jesus which the author could not
but insert, but which are in essential variance
with his own stiff and narrow conception of
the Church. This ecclesiasticism is held to
be evidenced by passages in which " the
world " is referred to as emphatically distinct
from, and hostile to, Christ and his disciples ;
by passages in which " those who are of the
truth " are regarded as wholly separate from
those who are not of the truth, " the sheep "
who hear the voice of the shepherd from those

who do not or cannot hear his voice ; by passages in the farewell discourses where Jesus prays " not for the world but for them which thou hast given me." " His own " are thus regarded as those who belong to the institution, who have rendered intellectual assent to its doctrinal statements.

This view, I say, I regard as dictated by the presupposition that the Gospel is an ecclesiastical and theological document. If, on the contrary, it is regarded from the standpoint here maintained, all such passages will be seen to be expressive, not of an *a priori* separatism of rigorous ecclesiasticism, but of the *experienced fact* that some responded to Jesus and some did not, that some heard his voice and some did not, that some were his friends and some were not. The author is neither concerned with the question of an " ecclesiastically elect," nor with the question of a " theologically predestined." He is concerned with the fact of the division which the presence of Jesus created, and with what may be called the spiritual and moral conditionality of faith. He says in his own way and with his own dramatic emphasis—or over-emphasis—what in the Synoptic Gospels is continually being said : " For narrow is the gate, and straitened the way, that leadeth unto life, and few be they that find it " (Matt. vii. 14) ; " Strive to enter in by the narrow door ; for many, I say unto you, shall seek to enter in, and shall not be able " (Lk. xiii. 24) ; " that seeing they may not see, and hearing they may not understand " (Lk. viii. 10, and parallel passages). No more than the Synoptists does the Johannine author intend either to say himself or to make Jesus say that the way to salvation is only for those inside an institution, or for those who un-critically acquiesce in dogma, or for a few elect souls. He is expressing the mind of Jesus whose mission and message were to all, though all would not hear and obey.[1]

[1] As an example of an interpretation of the Gospel, which sees in it a narrow, exclusive ecclasiasticism, I refer the reader to Dr. E. F. Scott's book already cited. See especially Chapter iv. The Evangelist, he says, " has learned to identify Christianity with the Church as an outward institution " (p. 116). " It is here that John makes his gravest departure from the actual message of Christ as we know it in the Synoptic Gospels " (*ibid*.). The " beloved disciple " to Dr. Scott, signifi-cantly enough, " represents the Church in its essential

ETERNAL LIFE.

This whole doctrine of man reaches its consummation in the Johannine message of *eternal life*. From what has already been said the essential nature of this life should be manifest. It is a life of quality, not of quantity ; of timeless reality, not of temporal existence. This Gospel affords no support to materialistic views of a magical impartation of " immortality." Neither does it contain any doctrine of " heaven " and " hell " which would gratify the endeavours of cosmic geographers. The whole conception is on the loftiest plane of spiritual communion and ethical endeavour.

In the Nicodemus discourse in chapter three, Jesus declares to Nicodemus that the entrance to this life is by a new birth. " Except a man be born anew, he cannot see the king-

idea " (p. 144). My whole interpretation of the Gospel is an answer to this view of the author's mind and intention. It is interesting to note that " Catholic " interpreters of the Gospel see the same type of ecclesiastical mind behind it as Dr. E. F. Scott sees : only, in their case, there is, of course, whole-hearted approval of such an ecclesiasticism.

dom of God " (v. 3). Nicodemus had known
that Jesus was a teacher come from God, but
this " knowledge " had to be quickened into
" spirit " by the Divine Spirit. " That which
is born of flesh is flesh, that which is born of
Spirit is spirit " (v. 6). It is, that is, not
a creaturely existence compassed by temporal
and spatial limitations ; it is a participation
in the essential nature of God Himself.
Nicodemus cannot understand how these
things can be. Jesus replies that he speaks
from out the depth of his own experience.
" We speak that we do know, and bear witness
of that we have seen " (v. 11). Jesus is
then set forth as the medium of this life. The
perfection of his own sonship awakens this
experience in those who " believe on him."
He is the mediator of eternal life to all such
(vv. 15-17). But he is the mediator, because
of the experienced fact that eternal life was
in him ; it is not because he is the mediator
that eternal life flows from him. This whole
experiential approach is seen also in the discourse of the sixth chapter. Jesus claims
to be mediator of eternal life because of the
experienced fact that he expressed spiritual

reality, eternal life. " It is the spirit that quickeneth ; the flesh profiteth nothing : the words that I have spoken unto you are spirit, and are life " (v. 63). When he who is the " Word " speaks, the words he speaks are " spirit " and " life." To say, then, that Jesus is the " Word " is just another way of saying that eternal life dwells in him. To say that he is the medium of eternal life is to say that those who hear and receive in faith the Divine Word thereby partake of that life. The sustenance of this life in us, as in him, is in doing the will of the Divine Father. " My meat," Jesus says, " is to do the will of Him that sent me and to accomplish His work " (iv. 34). And to others Jesus says : " Work not for the meat which perisheth, but for the meat which abideth unto eternal life " (vi. 27). The Son gives to men this " meat " in so far as they eat it : to eat this " meat " is to do the will of God which he does perfectly.

All this is summed up in the prayer of Jesus as high priest in the seventeenth chapter. The reality throbbing through this sublime chapter is that of a consciousness of unique, but dependent, spiritual oneness with God ;